THE **BEST** DIGITAL MARKETING CAMPAIGNS IN THE WORLD

DAMIAN RYAN AND CALVIN JONES

THE **BEST** DIGITAL MARKETING CAMPAIGNS IN THE WORLD

MASTERING THE ART OF CUSTOMER ENGAGEMENT

KoganPage

LONDON PHILADELPHIA NEW DELHI

First published in Great Britain and the United States in 2011 by Kogan Page Limited

120 Pentonville Road	1518 Walnut Street, Suite 1100	4737/23 Ansari Road
London N1 9JN	Philadelphia PA 19102	Daryaganj
United Kingdom	USA	New Delhi 110002
www.koganpage.com		India

© Damian Ryan and Calvin Jones, 2011

ISBN   978 0 7494 6062 4
E-ISBN   978 0 7494 6063 1

British Library Cataloguing-in-Publication Data

A CIP record for this book is available from the British Library.

Library of Congress Cataloging-in-Publication Data

Ryan, Damian.
   The best digital marketing campaigns in the world : mastering the art of customer engagement / Damian Ryan, Calvin Jones.
      p. cm.
   Includes index.
      ISBN 978-0-7494-6062-4 – ISBN 978-0-7494-6063-1 1. Internet marketing–Case studies. 2. Advertising campaigns–Case studies. 3. Social media. 4. Marketing–Management. I. Jones, Calvin. II. Title.
   HF5415.1265.R92 2011
   658.8'72–dc22
                                                      2010053866

Typeset by Saxon Graphics Ltd
Printed and bound in India by Replika Press Pvt Ltd

CONTENTS

ACKNOWLEDGEMENTS

Damian Ryan

My deepest thanks and gratitude to my charming daughters (who have just launched their first magazine at the tender age of 7!), my family, friends and of course Calvin and Eva for their input. This book is dedicated to Fiona – a constant source of inspiration, friendship and love.

Calvin Jones

Writing any book is a collaborative process. That's especially true of a book like this, where as authors we were dependent on the readiness of others to share their information and insight with us. So a big collective thank you is due to the agency boss's, creative directors, brand managers and individuals who shared their work with us. You made this book possible.

Thanks also to Damian... it's been a pleasure working with you again, and to Eva, for making sense of the chaos and presenting us with a sensible, coherent body of material to work with. This was, in all ways, a team effort.

To my parents, Yvonne and Clive Jones... who I forgot to mention first time around... a very special thank you for everything.

Most of all thanks to Sal, Ava, Nia and Lana... my arch-collaborators in life. Well done guys... this work is every bit as much yours as it is mine.

INTRODUCTION

- 7.5 million – that's the number of results you get when you Google 'the best digital marketing campaigns in the world'.

- In second place (at the time of writing) is a mention of this book – that's not a bad start!

- Digital marketing – the fastest growth area of marketing we have ever witnessed – now competes for the lion's share of an annual pot worth approximately one trillion dollars (according to advertising giant WPP).

In 2009, our first book, *Understanding Digital Marketing* (UDM), hit the shelves. Since then it's been delivering a solid foundation of digital marketing know-how to practitioners around the world, and continues to do so.

We learnt a lot of valuable lessons during the writing process. Here are just a few.

Writing a book is far from easy. Although we were both very comfortable with the subject matter, and had plenty of experience and expertise to draw on, digital marketing refused to sit still. We felt a bit like portrait painters of old must have felt, trying desperately to recreate a reliable likeness of an impossibly restless child.

But when you're tackling a subject that's in a constant state of flux you're prepared for that. What we weren't prepared for was the ever-present, all-consuming nature of the process. It grows rapidly to become a roaring juggernaut that pervades every facet of your life, and that refuses to go away until the project is finished. It was an incredibly challenging, but at the same time very rewarding, experience.

UDM was an exciting project for us, and holding a copy of your first book in your hands is a real thrill – but more satisfying perhaps was the privilege of participating in a dynamic shift in thinking. Businesses around the world were embracing digital marketing and were seeing it deliver on at least some of its boundless promise.

People really like examples. That was one of the key themes that emerged as the feedback from the book flooded in. While UDM offers a comprehensive overview of the digital marketing space and the various opportunities digital presents for brands and businesses, the message from you, our readers, was that you wanted to see more examples of how brands and businesses were using these digital technologies and techniques to engage more effectively with their customers in the real world.

As marketers you wanted to see more case studies. While finely crafted chapters on web analytics and neatly woven prose explaining search engine optimization offered a necessary and useful foundation of digital marketing knowledge, marketers tend to have a strong interest in seeing how digital campaigns are constructed and how brands are applying the theory in real situations.

Another theme, particularly from those of you in the corporate sector, echoed the call for more case studies – but with the emphasis on delivering concrete examples to help 'sell' the merits of digital to your board. UDM helped to dispel some of the mystery and shared a foundation of digital knowledge, but you needed compelling stories of successful digital marketing campaigns that would spur your board into action.

Because digital marketing transcends traditional geographic boundaries, you also highlighted the need for more inclusive examples of digital being used effectively around the world, and not just from English-speaking markets. This was a sentiment particularly prominent among small advertisers and marketers looking to expand their reach using digital channels. It was also important to try and understand how the 'digital engagement channels' differed from market to market. The mix of channels you use to reach your market effectively in Japan, for example, is likely to be significantly different from the mix of channels you'd choose in Europe. While you might choose Facebook and Google to reach out to UK consumers, the same campaign could be better suited to mobile social networks in Korea.

While we engaged in this exchange of ideas – online, of course – something else happened that took us a little by surprise, but that was at the same time terribly digital. Marketers started to send us their case studies. Among them were those who genuinely wanted to share what they had learned from UDM, to show us how they had successfully applied the lessons in the book to achieve digital marketing success for themselves.

It served as a poignant reminder of the power and influence of the printed page in an age of all-consuming digital. Books remain an incredibly compelling and important medium, and will do for some time to come.

Faced with all of this input from readers we sat down together in mid-2009 at The Beehive Bar in Connonagh – a real Irish pub in the wilds of West Cork – to discuss how we could deliver what you were looking for. The ultimate outcome of that animated and creative conversation is this book.

The 25 case studies that follow are a sample of the best digital marketing campaigns of the past few years. Naturally this isn't an exhaustive list – not by a long chalk – nor is it meant to be. By its very nature this book was always going to be a subjective exercise. These are case studies we've found and researched over the past year or so, and inevitably the book carries with it an element of bias towards our own particular favourites. Another thing to bear in mind as you consider the examples that follow, and compare and contrast them with others that aren't included here, is that some of the case studies we really wanted to share with you simply weren't available to us. The agencies or brands concerned were, for reasons of their own, unable or unwilling to share the information we needed.

We also pondered long and hard on whether scoring or ranking the case studies – putting them in some sort of order of merit – would add value. Eventually it dawned on us that scoring would be a largely arbitrary exercise. Instead we decided to present the campaigns in no particular order and to let you decide which of them you prefer, and to suggest favourites of your own on www.understandingdigital.com, on Facebook (www.facebook.com/understandingdigital), on Twitter (@udigital) and through your own websites, blogs and social media channels.

This book, then, is a starting point. We're kick-starting a conversation with this selection of digital marketing case studies and examples, whetting our collective appetites and beginning what we hope will be an enduring online conversation from which we can all reap the benefits.

Selecting the campaigns

How did we choose which campaigns would feature in this book? It wasn't easy. To begin with we drew up a shortlist of more than 100 campaigns from a variety of sources. These included industry award nominations, campaigns that had generated significant levels of online buzz, submissions by readers of UDM and of course those campaigns that had really resonated with each of us over the past year or two.

Then we worked through the list, did a little digging and assessed them based on the following criteria.

Understanding the challenge and applying practical solutions

From the outset we wanted to see campaigns that didn't go crazy by creating unsustainable and awkward engagement models. We also looked for evidence that the agency completely understood both the product and the proposition, but more importantly had produced work that was relevant and practical to a digital world. Rather than see a digital strategy for the audience, we wanted to see a strategy for the digital audience – if that makes sense.

Innovation and clever use of technology

This is a throwback to when Damian created the Golden Spider Awards in 1997 and the Digital Media Awards in 2002 (both still giving gongs) – the same criteria were used then. Ultimately we were looking for something that pushed the digital boundaries by being achingly smart. Without reinventing the wheel we wanted something that made us wonder 'why hasn't anybody thought of that before?'

Creativity and presentation

This book is all about creativity, but it's how the campaign engaged us as readers, writers and digital marketers that really mattered. Later you will read opinions from several digital marketing experts who commented on some of the campaigns. While their opinions didn't necessarily reflect our own selection of the campaigns, we were mindful of how 'engaged' they did or didn't feel.

The standard of presentation was another important factor. Online and mobile channels impose certain creative constraints but also offer possibilities. What we wanted to see here was campaigns that made you sit up and perhaps even utter the magic words 'that's cool'!

Return on investment

While many still feel the internet is a direct response medium (most of them traditional agencies who are still lurking on the periphery of digital) and should be judged purely on percentiles and financial returns, others, ourselves included, feel a bit differently. Whether the return on investment (ROI) was in fact sales, profit, market share, new customers or brand awareness, we wanted to see engagement. In particular we wanted to see campaigns that emphasized engagement from the very outset and understood that digital marketing was a method to achieve this.

Overall level of brilliance

This is the overall 'wow!' factor – that unquantifiable something that reso-nates at a subconscious level. Ideally we wanted to see advertisers breaking the mould, especially if they were relatively new to digital marketing or trying new techniques.

Eva and the experts

That's not a bad name for a rock band – but in this case it was an oft-coined expression during the creative process behind the book.

When we decided to write something inclusive and global, we hit on the idea of inviting digital marketing experts from around the world to comment on some of the campaigns. We felt it was a really good way of adding an additional element of perspective to the content, and of keeping us in touch with the thoughts of leaders, thinkers and visionaries in this sector.

We were also faced with the onerous task of researching, collecting, collating and analysing more than 100 case studies. This was a completely different challenge to the original research for UDM; gathering case studies meant we were relying on receiving timely and accurate information from third parties – agencies and brands. Coordinating the process, ensuring that we got to the people we needed to speak to and that they delivered the information we needed, was always going to be a tall order. We knew early in the process that we'd need the help of a tenacious researcher who understood the digital space and had a passion for all things creative.

Enter Eva McLaughlin. Based in Amsterdam, Eva has spent the best part of a year hassling agencies and advertisers to divulge the information in the case studies that follow. Without her persistence and tenacity you wouldn't be holding this book today. So, a big thank you to Eva!

Understanding Digital: a personal view

Damian

Understanding Digital has been a continuous journey. It began 18 years ago when I first saw the internet in Jerry Reitman's office at Leo Burnett in Chicago. Being part of the greatest communications revolution in history is an exciting role, but I have always felt that you get out of it what you put into it. Maybe that's karma.

Although I no longer run an agency or media company my passion for this business has ensured I have remained at its heart. Following several years with corporate finance firm Results International Group (thanks to Graham, Keith, Andy and Co) I have now founded a specialist mergers and acquisition business for the digital media sector, www.mediaventura.com.

I believe the book and site and all the events and other stuff I do with Calvin will demonstrate my commitment to this space and help give a new breed of business something different to leverage and help to open doors in a highly competitive market.

As my father often says: 'it's not the principle it's the money'! He also says 'the fastest way to get a pig up the stairs is to pull it down by its tail' – these two guiding mantras help me in business life every single day, especially the latter.

Calvin

Damian calls Understanding Digital a continuous journey. In many ways I feel the same, but I tend to look at it as more of an ongoing adventure. Every day in the world of online marketing is different. It's dynamic, it's fast paced and occasionally it's overwhelming… but it's never dull.

That presents many challenges, but keeping abreast of the constant flux helps keep me on my toes and I hope pushes me to produce better work.

Of course, one of the best ways of keeping up with the staggering rate of change also turns out to be one of the most rewarding aspects of the work. Every day I'm privileged to engage with, and learn from, literally hundreds of amazing people: people from just around the corner and right across the world. You know who you are.

The connections I've made online and subsequently (in too few cases) face-to-face really are priceless. Working with Damian again has, of course, been as eventful, entertaining and thought provoking as ever!

Most of all though, writing a second book has allowed me to perpetuate the notion that all of the time I spend on Twitter, Facebook, Foursquare, watching YouTube videos and playing with iPhone apps is, in fact, real work. Long may it last!

The case studies that follow offer some amazing examples of what's possible, but as we mentioned earlier they're not exhaustive by any means. New creative opportunities and innovation are everywhere online, and some very bright people are constantly thinking up new ways to explore the possibilities. This is, and was only ever going to be, a snapshot.

By their nature case studies from big brands and agencies are more prominent and accessible than smaller campaigns. That's the main reason the bulk of the case studies that follow fall into that category, but we believe there are lessons to be drawn from each of them that can inspire and inform businesses of all sizes.

These case studies offer, as we've already mentioned, a starting point for discussion. Now it's your turn to let us know what you think – contact us at www.understandingdigital.com, @UDigital on Twitter and on www.facebook.com/UnderstandingDigital.

See you online…

We hope this book helps to share the hard-earned knowledge and skill of some of the world's top digital creative minds. We hope it convinces businesses large and small to invest more in digital marketing and to take a longer-term view of its power and potential to transform their business. Above all we hope it helps you to sell more and increase profits while finding more effective and manageable ways to engage your community in dynamic and enduring relationships.

THE RAPID EVOLUTION OF (DIGITAL) MARKETING

Human nature has a tendency to admire complexity but reward simplicity.

Ben Huh, CEO, Cheezburger Network, addressing the SMX East conference in October 2009

Things move quickly online. New services spring up practically overnight, and trends shift at the drop of a (virtual) hat. As online marketers we're on a constant learning curve, one that usually gets steeper the higher up it we manage to climb. Keeping on top of everything that's going on in the digital space is difficult – we know, we live and breathe it every day, and there's always new stuff to learn. It can be overwhelming, but it's important to take a step back, a deep breath, and to look at the bigger picture. When you tear yourself away from the day-to-day minutiae you'll find definite macro-trends emerging that will help you as you embark on your next digital marketing adventure.

Your business, your brand, your customers – a unique combination

Search online or browse a bookshelf on anything to do with internet marketing and you'll find reams of prescriptive formulas and 'how to' guides promising instant success. We've never been fans of prescriptive formulae, and here's why: anything that's general enough to 'work' across the board patently doesn't. By definition a one-size-fits-all solution is generic; it's not tailored to your business's unique needs and so it cannot possibly deliver the best results for your business. Unless somebody knows your business, your customers and your market inside out how can they possibly offer you step-by-step instructions that will work seamlessly in your particular circumstances?

The short answer is that they cannot – and neither can we.

What we can do, however, is explore some of the trends that have emerged in the digital marketing space over the past couple of years, examine where we are today and then, in the case studies that follow, show you how some of the world's leading brands are using digital marketing to engage more effectively with audiences, promote brand awareness and boost their bottom line.

Where are we now?

As authors we're very conscious that any book about digital marketing, including this one, is in danger of dating quickly. The topic is among the most fluid and dynamic imaginable, and continues to evolve at a mind-boggling pace. Tools and services appear online seemingly overnight, and many disappear just as quickly, waxing and waning to the rhythm of fickle online consumers. All of which makes it a very exciting field to be involved in, but also makes writing about it in a way that will retain value for you, the reader, a challenging endeavour to say the least. But then, we're always up for a challenge.

It's a huge and still rapidly growing market

As we were researching *Understanding Digital Marketing* in early 2008, global online population statistics (www.internetworldstats.com) put the number of internet users worldwide at about 1.3 billion. The latest stats, as of 30 June 2010, showed that close to 2 billion people across the globe had regular access to the internet. That's an additional 700,000 people or so, give or take a few million, in just a couple of years, and means that today more than a quarter of the global population has access to the internet. Consider the regional breakdown of internet penetration and you start to see just how crucial it is for your business to connect with its customers online, wherever in the world you happen to operate.

In North America more than 77 per cent of people are online, in Australasia/ Oceania it's 61 per cent and in Europe 77 per cent – although within that subdued European figure of just over half you have Scandinavian states sporting 80–95 per cent penetration, and the UK with more than 82 per cent. Asia's internet penetration figures stand at around 21.5 per cent, but that doesn't give the full picture either, because there's a massive swing from a high 81.1 per cent penetration in South Korea to a very low 0.4 per cent penetration in Bangladesh. Percentages can hide the sheer scale of the potential online market in some of these countries too.

Take China as an example. Only 31.6 per cent of Chinese people have internet access. That doesn't sound like much, but translate it to actual individual internet users and it represents a massive 420,000,000 people, giving China the world's largest online population by quite some margin.

A global phenomenon, local impact

In its report *Top Predictions for IT Organizations and Users, 2010 and Beyond: A New Balance*, analyst firm Gartner predicts that by 2014 more than 3 billion people – or a significant majority of the world's adult population – will have the ability to 'transact electronically via mobile or Internet technologies'. That's a staggering statistic that represents a fundamental shift in the foundation of global commerce.

Widespread internet adoption and the use of electronic media to facilitate commerce is a global phenomenon, but it's one that even local businesses cannot afford to ignore. Whether people are looking for a plumber to fit their new bathroom suite or using a smartphone to pinpoint peer-recommended Italian restaurants near where they're staying, consumers rely on the internet to guide their international, national and local purchasing decisions. Ready or not, that's already having an impact on your business.

The way we access and use the internet is changing

Once upon a time, not so very long ago, almost everyone who accessed the internet was doing so through a fixed desktop computer hooked up to either a work network or a painfully slow dial-up modem at home. These days the desktop PC is still with us, but you'll also find wireless-enabled laptops and even more portable netbooks offering untethered access to high-speed, wireless internet from anywhere in the home and beyond.

Access to always-on broadband is becoming almost ubiquitous in the developed world (although there are still a few exceptions, as I'm reminded writing this in rural Ireland). Using the internet today has become so quick and convenient for many of us that we're going online more often, staying online for longer and doing much more online than we ever have before.

Going social

The shift towards social media is perhaps the most significant recent development in online marketing. Who hasn't heard about the meteoric rise of Facebook to the top of the social networking tree or the explosive growth of Twitter during 2009?

In April 2010, UK internet users spent 65 per cent more time online (884 million hours) than they did in April 2007 (536 million hours), according to figures from the UK Online Measurement company (UKOM) (nielsenwire, June 2010). The same report reveals a huge shift towards social media, showing that in 2007, social networks and blogs accounted for less than 9 per cent of all UK internet time, while in 2010, social sites and blogs accounted for nearly 23 per cent of the total time UK internet users spend online.

'Despite the large increase in the amount of time people spend online and the increasing proliferation of websites and online services, one thing has remained constant, and that is the bulk of time accounted for by communicating, networking and playing games,' says Alex Burmaster, Vice President of Global Communications for Nielsen's online division. 'These are the pillars on which the internet as a heavily used medium are built.'

What we do online: UK internet usage for April 2010 condensed into one hour (source: UKOM/nielsen).

If all April 2010 UK internet time was condensed into one hour, how much time would be spent in the most heavily used sectors?

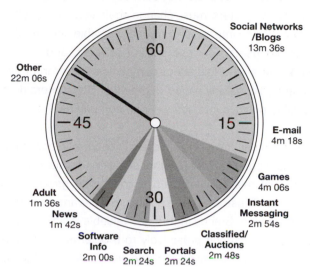

Social Networks /Blogs 13m 36s

Other 22m 06s

E-mail 4m 18s

Games 4m 06s

Adult 1m 36s

Instant Messaging 2m 54s

News 1m 42s

Software Info 2m 00s

Search 2m 24s

Portals 2m 24s

Classified/ Auctions 2m 48s

Source: UKOM

Social media is not only changing the way people communicate online, but is impacting the way they consume other media too – people are using their online social connections to filter, discuss, disseminate and validate the news, entertainment and products they choose to consume, online and offline.

In June 2010, eMarketer reported that social networks in the United States had reached what it described as 'critical mass'. The company estimated that 57.5 per cent of all US internet users (some 127 million people) would use a social network at least once a month in 2010. By 2014, it estimated that almost two-thirds of US internet users would be using social networks regularly.

But are consumers really interested in connecting with brands on sites where, historically, it's always been more about friends interacting with friends?

According to eMarketer senior analyst Debra Aho Williamson they definitely are.

'Those who still think that social network users are too busy engaging with friends to notice marketers must change their viewpoint,' she said on the company's blog. 'Brand interactions are real, valuable and growing. More than half of all internet users now use social networks, and the percentage of social network users who talk about companies, either in organic conversations or on branded company pages, is growing. Consumers do pay attention and they do value positive interactions with companies.'

Brands large and small are using Twitter, Facebook, blogs, forums, content sharing, bookmarking, reviews and other social media sites to foster ongoing, mutually beneficial relationships with a constantly growing community of online consumers. These are people who really want to engage with their favourite brands online. Brands in turn get valuable insight into what customers really want, can respond proactively to problems as soon as they arise, add value and notify people who are genuinely interested about new products, offers, events or whatever, enhancing the overall customer experience and boosting their online reputation.

Used effectively, social media is a great example of a win–win, with customers and brands benefiting in equal measure from the interaction.

How big is social media?

At the time of writing, Facebook is king of the social media heap. According to its own stats page it had more than 500 million active users, 50 per cent of whom logged on to Facebook on any given day. People on the site interacted with 160 million objects (pages, groups and events). The average Facebook user, the company said, connected to 60 pages, groups and events, and created 70 pieces of content each month. In total, more than 25 billion pieces of content (links, news stories, blog posts, notes, photo albums, etc) were being shared on Facebook every month.

In March 2010, the competitive intelligence service Hitwise recorded Facebook pulling ahead of Google for the first time ever as the most visited website in the United States. In May 2010, it did the same thing in the UK. Facebook is huge, it's growing all the time and the steady evolution of Facebook pages for businesses has been a catalyst for brands to harness what Facebook does best: interaction and engagement.

Twitter is also big news, and while its user base is much lower than that of Facebook, it continues to grow at an astonishing rate. Here are some of the stats the micro-blogging service shared during its 'Chirp' Developer Conference in San Francisco on 14 April 2010:

- Twitter has 105,779,710 registered users.
- New users are signing up at the rate of 300,000 per day.
- 180 million unique visitors come to the site every month.
- 75 per cent of Twitter traffic comes from outside Twitter.com (ie via third-party applications).
- Twitter gets a total of 3 billion requests a day via its application programming interface (API).
- Twitter users are, in total, tweeting an average of 55 million tweets per day.
- Twitter's search engine receives around 600 million search queries per day.
- Of Twitter's active users, 37 per cent use their phone to tweet.
- Over half of all tweets (60 per cent) come from third-party applications.
- Twitter as a business has grown: in the past year it has grown from 25 to 175 employees.

Those are impressive numbers, but it's important to remember that the big players in social media don't represent the only game in town. There are thousands of specialist social media sites out there catering for enthusiasts in every niche market imaginable. While they don't have the scope or reach of the bigger sites, they do have something potentially more valuable to your business: relevance.

As always in online marketing, it pays to do your homework, to find out what's out there. You need to know what the people you want to connect with are talking about, and where. Look at the available options and decide where you can best contribute constructively to the online dialogue to ultimately win and retain business.

Going mobile

As well as shifting usage patterns, we're also accessing the internet today using a broader array of devices than ever before: from digital set-top-boxes to games consoles, the family PC to sophisticated mobile phones and the latest dedicated internet-optimized devices, 'tablets' such as Apple's much vaunted iPad™, designed to make accessing the web easier, more convenient and more compelling than ever.

In most developing nations personal mobile devices are the primary mode of internet access today, and according to Gartner's analysts, by 2013 browser-enabled mobile phones will overtake PCs as the most common web access device worldwide. They predict there will be 1.78 billion PCs in use in 2013, compared to 1.82 billion browser-equipped mobiles. Mobiles will continue to outnumber PCs for internet access thereafter.

Mobile commerce is set to rise accordingly, with the widespread adoption of web-enabled smartphones, affordable mobile data plans over existing 3G and emerging 4G mobile networks and the maturing of mobile payment gateways. US technology research company Coda Research Consultancy Ltd predicts a doubling of mobile commerce revenues in the United States during 2010. As consumers overcome their initial reluctance to paying for things using their mobiles, they'll spend a projected US $2.4 billion for the year (eMarketer.com, June 2010).

Meanwhile PriceGrabber.com's 'Smartphone Shopping Behaviour Report' reveals that in April 2010, 35 per cent of US web-enabled mobile phone users said they had participated in shopping-related activity (including browsing and researching prospective purchases) on their mobile phones over the past year.

Mobile internet usage is gaining traction and is starting to fulfil some of its long-anticipated promise as 'the next big thing' in digital marketing. If you want to stay ahead of the game, your digital marketing strategy needs to evolve to encompass mobile-optimized content for easy access on small form-factor devices. Mobile-specific applications and campaigns also need to form part of your online marketing mix moving forward, and many of the case studies you'll read later in the book include a mobile element.

Embracing and facilitating mobile internet access for your brand is an intelligent step today… and will become an imperative for online success for many businesses over the coming years.

Any time, any place, anywhere

Thanks to the ubiquity of broadband in the home, the widespread availability of public WiFi hotspots, better 3G mobile coverage and more affordable mobile data plans, internet access really is becoming an any time, anywhere commodity. It's cheap, it's convenient and it's changing the way we communicate and interact on a social and a commercial level.

As marketers, we need to be aware of these changes, understand them and adapt to them. We have a remarkable opportunity to harness the potential of this shift in consumer behaviour to connect with customers in a more targeted way that adds real value, instead of merely pumping out messages that few of them really want to hear.

Of course, instant access to the internet whenever and wherever people go means that they are tweeting, updating, reviewing and generally commenting on their daily experiences as they happen. Anyone on Twitter knows that most of the major international, national and local news stories of 2009/2010 broke on the short messaging/micro-blogging service long before 'traditional' media channels got wind of them.

That immediacy doesn't just apply to news: that bad experience in a restaurant, poor customer service on the telephone or frustration at an ineffective product is now spreading online as soon as it happens in all its multimedia glory. That makes the quest for excellence, and the need to offer customers real service and value, more crucial than ever. It also means that brands need to be extra vigilant when it comes to monitoring online sentiment and engaging proactively in the online communities where their customers choose to spend their time.

Location, location, location

Coupled to a large degree with the growing number of high-end mobiles, many of them equipped with built-in GPS receivers, and the refinement of methods to determine the approximate position of non-GPS-enabled mobile phones, is the rise of location-based services.

These services allow users to access (and businesses/marketers to deliver) relevant information (and targeted advertising) directly to their handsets based on their current location.

That could be a GPS-enabled smartphone app that automatically routes your takeaway order to the nearest restaurant of your favourite pizza chain, making sure your pizza arrives piping hot in the shortest possible time; a service that delivers regular weather updates for your current location, wherever you happen to be in the world; or one that lets you see which of your online friends is nearby, so you can arrange an impromptu face-to-face meet up.

Location-aware social applications such as FourSquare (www.foursquare. com) allow people to discover new places wherever they go, 'check in' and see who else is at the same venue or at other venues nearby, read tips and recommendations from people who have been to the same venue before, and earn points, badges and other virtual and real-world goodies for regular visits to the same venue.

Foursquare allows people to discover new places, see which of their friends are nearby and connect with others based on their current location.

For marketers, location-aware services offer the opportunity to connect with customers who are physically nearby – offering timely, valuable information and new ways to connect through rewards, incentives and more. Many bars and restaurants, for example, are already offering discounts and rewards to regular FourSquare visitors to their establishments.

Location-based marketing is in its infancy, but is certainly growing fast as sales of location-aware mobile phones continue to accelerate. We're only beginning to tap into its potential. Whether location-based marketing offers great opportunities for your business or not will depend largely on what you do and who your customers are, but it's certainly something to bear in mind as you ponder your strategy moving forward.

Say it with (moving) pictures

If a picture is worth a thousand words, how much is video worth? Quite a lot, as it happens.

Online video has been around for some time now and is already a well-utilized marketing channel in its own right, but it's one that continues to grow apace, and the rise of the viral video shows no sign of abating any time soon. During April 2010 around 178 million US internet users watched 30.3 billion online videos, that's according to the latest figures from comScore. In December 2008 comScore also published figures that showed that video-sharing giant YouTube (which is owned by Google) had surpassed Yahoo! to become the *second most popular search engine on the internet* in its own right, after Google's own core search service, a spot it has retained ever since.

Online video is so powerful because well-executed video can be incredibly engaging and entertaining, demands little effort to consume and packs a lot of information into a relatively short space of time in comparison to other media. It's also incredibly easy to share, so people do, all the time, through social media, blogs, e-mail, etc.

Viral video, often distributed via Google's video-sharing site YouTube, has become a stalwart of contemporary online marketing campaigns.

Video is a firmly entrenched stalwart of the online marketers toolkit today, and you'll find viral video components featuring in many of the case studies later in this book.

Don't forget the old faithful

All of these changes give you a flavour of the shifting sands of the digital marketing landscape, but lest we forget, the basics of online marketing – developing a solid strategy, creating a high-quality web presence, search engine optimization (SEO) and search engine marketing (SEM), website analytics, e-mail marketing, social media, online PR, affiliate marketing and online display advertising, the topics we cover in *Understanding Digital Marketing* – all still apply. Effective digital marketing is all about finding the blend of channels that works best for your particular business and your particular group of customers.

Amidst all the media coverage and online hype surrounding social media, it's easy to forget that search offers the most effective direct channel to targeted prospects who are actively looking for what you have to sell. According to comScore figures for December 2009, the global search market grew by 46 per cent year on year, with a staggering 131.3 billion searches conducted worldwide during the course of that single month, compared to 89.7 billion searches for December 2008.

We mentioned this in the first chapter of *Understanding Digital Marketing* and it's worth reiterating here.

Technological advances have punctuated the evolution of advertising throughout history, each fundamentally altering the way businesses could communicate with their customers. Interestingly, however, none of these ground-breaking developments superseded those that came before. Rather, they served to augment them, offering marketers more diversity, allowing them to connect with a broader cross-section of consumers. In today's sophisticated age of paid search placement, keyword-targeted pay-per-click advertising and social networking, you'll still find the earliest forms of advertising alive and well.

That assertion applies equally to digital channels. Popular emerging platforms in the digital space don't supplant the channels we're already using, they simply add more strings to the online marketer's virtual bow, offering ever more opportunities to reach out to and engage with consumers and business customers.

The case studies that follow help to illustrate how some familiar brands, and one or two less familiar ones, are rising to the challenges thrown up by today's digital marketing landscape. Leading marketers offer us a glimpse into an eclectic mix of campaigns that have been particularly successful over the past few years, and provide inspiration, ideas and insight that will help us with our own campaigns in turn.

Enjoy!

CASE STUDY I

DOCKERS 'PANTS DANCE'

The challenge

Dockers is a casual clothing brand owned by iconic US company Levi Strauss & Co. In early 2009, the company launched a brand revitalization campaign designed to put the Dockers brand front and centre in the minds of active, professional, tech-savvy males.

Campaign budget

US $100,000.

Target audience

Fashion-conscious consumers in the 18–45 age range, skewing male.

Action

Working closely with media communications specialist OMD's Ignition Factory and Dockers' creative agency Razorfish, Medialets, a rich media mobile platform for native mobile applications, developed a concept to deliver the world's first 'Shakeable ad' to the burgeoning iPhone market – a market that dovetailed perfectly with Dockers' demographic goals.

Dubbed 'Shakedown 2 Get Down', the ad featured Dufon, aka Orb/Orbit/Orbitron, a freestyle dance expressionist from a Seattle group called Circle of Fire. In the ad, Dufon dances around the screen wearing Dockers Vintage Workwear Khakis. The ad was built by the Medialets team and was served dynamically via their own ad-server into a number of high-profile iPhone apps, including the popular iBowl, i.TV, SGN Golf and iBasketball. It ran as a full-screen interstitial ad and included stop motion video, sound and the all-important 'Shakeable' interaction to move between dance sequences.

Results

This was a campaign designed purely to enhance brand recognition and awareness among the target demographic. There was no click-through action to drive traffic to a landing page of any sort; the campaign's goal was to encourage interaction and to engage with consumers in a completely new and innovative way.

The success of the campaign was measured by comparing engagement metrics such as average time per interaction of 42 seconds for the Dockers campaign compared with an average of just 12 seconds for online rich media advertising (source: Doubleclick), and an interaction rate of 33 per cent for the Dockers campaign compared to an 8 per cent average for rich media mobile content (source: insight express) and just 4.5 per cent for online rich media.

'Time per interaction' engagement metrics for the Dockers' pants-dance ad.

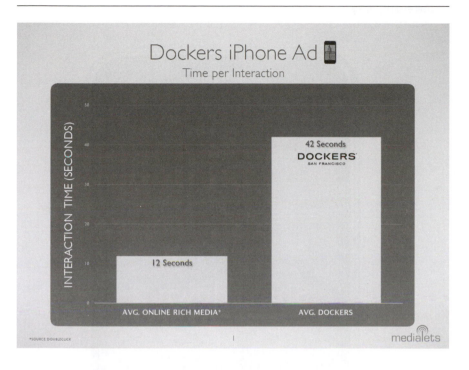

Lessons

The campaign is a great example of how knowing your audience and tailoring a campaign that delivers engaging content in an innovative way through the appropriate channel can resonate with consumers and deliver above-average results for brands. The way Dockers and Medialets tapped into the rapidly growing iPhone market, chose to serve their ads on iPhone apps that were popular with their target demographic (mainly sports games) and harnessed one of the iPhone's innovative features (the accelerometer that allows the device to measure and react to movement), all combined to deliver a unique campaign that resonated with their audience.

The Dockers iPhone app used the device's built-in accelerometer to let users interact with the campaign creative in an innovative and entertaining way.

Marketers, pay attention to the power of engagement – think about the wasted investment in newspaper ads that people ignore, television commercials aimed at people who would rather jump up and stick on the kettle, and direct mail masterpieces that go straight in the bin. It is one thing knowing your audience, but holding their attention in an invitational and non-intrusive manner at least gives you a chance to get your message across without the same audience feeling as if they are being held to ransom.

It's OK to sell stuff and have some fun too!

Links to campaign creative

- http://www.medialets.com/campaignentry/ (interactive demo, full functionality requires Apple Safari v.4 or higher)

- http://www.youtube.com/watch?v=NwnuwGhcpRU (YouTube video of the iPhone ad in action)

An expert view

Jon Walsh, Partner, Media Ventures (Europe) Ltd

This Levi's campaign is totally original, using fantastic stop motion video mixed with the innovative utilization of the iPhone's accelerometer. The media selected and route to market of the mobile phone are perfect.

However, as a consumer I would feel that I'm being left short changed if there is an end to my 'Dockers journey' after the dance videos had been watched. Why can't I learn the dance moves, find out more about 'Circle of Fire', find the nearest Dockers store to where I am, upload my own (poor) attempts to imitate the moves? Levi's has effectively ended the conversation with the consumer when they don't need to.

In summary, great creative, great targeting on perfect medium, but lacking two-way engagement opportunity and relationship-building opportunity.

Jon Walsh, Partner, Media Ventures.

About Jon

Jon Walsh is a digital media specialist and entrepreneur. He is currently a partner at Media Ventures, a digital media investment vehicle, and a director at Mobile Ventures, a mobile ad sales start-up. More information at www.mobventures.com

Credits

Client	● Dockers San Francisco
Geographical scope	● Global
Agencies	● Medialets in association with OMD and Razorfish
	● Creative director: Theo Skye
Awards	● OMMA Finalist Mobile Marketing Campaign (World's First Shakeable Ad)
	● MIXX 2009 Silver for Mobile Platforms

Creative biography

Theo Skye

Theo Skye is the Creative Director and founding member of Medialets, the rich media mobile platform for native mobile applications. He invents new ad formats and develops creative and design strategies for top-tier mobile ad campaigns enabling brands to leverage the unique engagement opportunities available on today's mobile devices.

Prior to Medialets, Theo was immersed in the online world as a web strategy and design consultant in the Washington DC area. He offered the full gamut of web-related services from designing and running usability testing seminars with VeriSign to designing and single-handedly building entire web content management systems for the National Archives and Records Administration. He credits his graphic design background for his ability to creatively iterate through any challenge.

Theo lives in Brooklyn, New York, and works in Manhattan.

CASE STUDY 2

THE TRUTH ABOUT SMART

The challenge

Most people think they know all about the smart fortwo. They know it's a cute-looking two-seater that is easy to park and nippy around town. But because of its compact size and 'cute' form factor, people also tend to assume that the smart lacks 'real car' credentials. Common misconceptions are that the smart will be cramped on the inside, that the boot/trunk space will be practically non-existent and that something so small would be sure to crumple horribly in an accident.

Built by Mercedes-Benz, the smart fortwo actually measures up incredibly well against many of its much larger automotive rivals. Its front seats are bigger than those found in many executive saloons, the boot/trunk is big enough to transport a washing machine, and the unique 'Tridion' safety cell will survive the weight of around 400 elephants. All in a car that's packed with the very latest automotive technology.

Mercedes-Benz wanted to challenge the public's misconceptions about their ultra-compact vehicle. 'The truth about smart' was an online campaign designed to harness the interactive nature of online media to do exactly that.

Campaign budget

US $120,000.

Target audience

Predominantly young couples aged 20–35 living in the city.

Action

The campaign utilized a combination of rich media advertising and a dedicated rich media microsite (www.truthaboutsmart.co.uk) to highlight 'the truth about smart', and to resoundingly dispel widely held misconceptions about crucial areas such as comfort, safety, space, fuel economy and features.

The theme of the campaign was all about exposing the truth, and to drive that message home the microsite needed to feel very honest. So while it did use rich media to immerse the visitor in a dynamic and entertaining experience that includes video and audio, it did so without the flashy techno-gimmickry you'd generally associate with automotive websites. Instead it embraced a simple, clean design, and featured a down-to-earth, engaging narrator with a warm tone of voice and an amiable manner to lead people through the site.

A series of interactive sections prompted site visitors for their opinions about certain aspects of the smart fortwo through a number of multiple choice questions. The site also highlighted previous responses based on the last 10 visitors to the site, allowing the current participant to gauge other people's perception of the compact car.

Once the visitor had answered all the questions in a given section the narrator would point out any wrong answers and highlight misconceptions about the car.

Results

The site received more than 270,000 visitors within four months of launch and visitors stayed on the site for an average time of more than 4 minutes.

With a very low level of media spend the campaign generated an impressive 2,113 requests for further information on smart cars during its first four months.

Lessons

The results show the potential of a skilfully crafted digital campaign to harness negative misconceptions or preconceptions about a brand and to re-educate consumers in a positive way. The campaign highlights how the innovative application of interactive rich media, applied in a focused and considered way, can work effectively to engage and inform.

The aim of this campaign from the outset was to surprise and delight people about a car that was already a talking point by revealing truthful, unburnished facts about it in an entertaining and engaging way. That was certainly achieved, but there was also potential to embrace people's shifting perceptions and opinions and build on them by integrating with relevant social platforms. Doing so would have encouraged discussion and facilitated viral propagation of the campaign through social media channels, and promoted broader online conversations about the microsite and the smart brand among online friends.

A small car with big credentials: the truth about smart website.

Links to campaign creative

- http://www.truthaboutsmart.co.uk/

Credits

Client	• Mercedes Benz UK/smart
Geographical scope	• United Kingdom
Agencies	• Agency Republic (www.agencyrepublic.com) • Campaign contact: Jim Stump
Awards	• BIMA Award Runner-up for Advertising Microsite

CASE STUDY 3

DORITOS HOTEL 626

The challenge

Every year around Halloween, Doritos brings back two flavours of the popular chip from its flavour graveyard. This campaign was designed to honour that 'return from the dead' with an entertaining and simultaneously disquieting experience for their teenage consumers. With no budget for traditional media spend the main challenge was to create an experience so intense and innovative that teens would pass it around on their own.

Campaign budget

Less than US $500,000.

Target audience

The principal target audience for the campaign was 16- to 24-year-old males.

Action

To create a buzz around the resurrection of the Doritos flavours, Goodbody, Silverstein & Partners capitalized on the Halloween theme and set about creating an online experience with one goal in mind: to scare teenage Americans out of their wits.

Hotel 626 grabbed a demographic obsessed with horror films by their vivid imaginations and immersed them in a living nightmare where they became the star. Employing innovative live action techniques and first-person 3D animation never before seen on a website, visitors to the site found themselves trapped inside a haunted hotel facing a series of spine-chilling challenges to earn their freedom. Some of the challenges included photographing a psychopathic maid, singing a demon baby to sleep and escaping a madman's cell alive.

To make the experience even more personal Hotel 626 cleverly blurred the lines between the virtual world of the game and the real world in ways that had never been attempted before. Early in the game it used the player's webcam to surreptitiously snap a photo of them, and then featured their face prominently in the lair of a serial killer later in the gaming experience. The site also called players up on their mobile phone during game-play, offering tips on finding a way out of Hotel 626, but also causing a disquieting sense that somehow the denizens of the hotel already knew your every move.

Visitors could only play the game at night: Hotel 626 only opened its doors between the hours of 6pm and 6am, boosting the scare factor.

Spooky! Players could only access Dorito's Hotel 626 online game at night.

Hotel 626 on location

The video for the campaign was shot in an abandoned mental hospital outside Stockholm, Sweden. When the production team arrived they found 'bloody' handprints on their hotel room showers – a welcome message from the team at B-Reel who were working on the shoot (http://bit.ly/e5CnUh).

The run-down state of the hospital worked perfectly, and there was little need to dress any of the sets. One night after shooting had finished the security guard heard footsteps. He investigated, but couldn't find anyone. According to locals former patients often return to sleep in the hospital's basement.

Most of the shoot took place indoors, but one shot needed to be outside at night. But this was Stockholm in the middle of the summer. Real 'night' only descended at around 1.30 am, and only lasted about an hour – adding another quirky challenge for the team.

Results

Hotel 626 is a classic example of how really compelling content can propagate virally across the social web. Without paid advertising the site was featured on countless blogs, shared across video and social networking sites, and gained widespread media exposure. The success of the campaign was measured by the number of visits, the time spent on the site and the volume of media coverage generated through the Send to a Friend feature, YouTube postings, Facebook and Twitter updates.

In total the site lured more than 12 million visitors from 188 countries down the spooky hallways of Hotel 626 for an average stay of 13 minutes apiece – or nearly four times the industry average. Results on the ground were equally impressive: Doritos' 'resurrected' Halloween flavours sold out in stores within three weeks of launch.

Client testimonial

'We are thrilled that Hotel 626 provided an experience that people around the world enjoyed. The Doritos brand truly focuses on providing its fans with intense, one-of-a-kind experiences that allow us to engage with them in unique ways, and we felt Hotel 626 provided an opportunity to do just that. Many thanks to all of our partners that helped create such a ground-breaking site, but our greatest thanks go to the fans that have supported Hotel 626 and inspired us to continue creating online experiences that stretch beyond traditional creative limits.'

Rudy Wilson, Director of Marketing, Doritos

Lessons

Described by online commentators as 'unique' and 'innovative', the Doritos Hotel 626 campaign certainly harnessed the potential of rich media to deliver a truly engaging and immersive experience for site visitors. While perhaps not everybody's cup of tea, the campaign was skilfully tailored to appeal to the target demographic and by harnessing technology to blur the lines between the game and real life it created a real buzz within online communities.

Goodby, Silverstein & Partners took the lessons learnt from Hotel 626 and went on to 'make the scare more personal' in Asylum 626, where they did even more to blur the line between the virtual and real-world experience.

Of course not everyone has the budget to develop ground-breaking online gaming experiences involving lots of bespoke development, overseas video shoots and the like. But one of the beauties of digital is that it lowers the barriers to entry for creating compelling, tailored and interactive content considerably.

Really understanding your audience and creating imaginative content that resonates with them is a critical component of any online marketing campaign. But if you can take things one step further and trigger the inherent desire we all have to share 'cool' stuff with our friends, you're on to a real winner. That's something that's clearly demonstrated by the success of this campaign.

The Doritos Hotel 626 microsite.

Links to campaign creative

- http://hotel626.com

Credits

Client	• Frito-Lay
Geographical scope	• United States
Agencies	• Goodby, Silverstein & Partners, San Francisco • Creative directors: Hunter Hindman and Rick Condos • Site development: B-Reel, New York
Awards	• One of *Contagious Magazine*'s 'Most Contagious' pieces of 2008 • FWA's People's Choice Award 2008 • AdCritic's Most Viewed Interactive Item 2008 • Gold One Show Pencil – Brand Gaming Category • Gold One Show Pencil – Product-specific Microsite • Yellow D&AD Pencil – Websites/Microsites • Gold Cannes Lion – Cyber Category • Bronze Clio – Consumer-targeted Site • Bronze ANDY – Digital Category • New York Festivals Grand Award – Best Microsite • Webby – Food and Beverage Category

Creative biographies

Rick Condos and Hunter Hindman

Rick Condos, Executive Creative Director and Associate Partner
Rick rejoined Goodby, Silverstein & Partners in 2007 after spending two years at Wieden + Kennedy Amsterdam as Creative Director on Coca-Cola. His work on Coca-Cola garnered global acclaim, most notably for the Coke Side of Life launch and 'Happiness Factory'. Throughout his career he has created award-winning work for HP, Nike, Frito-Lay, *The Economist*, Bass Ale and many other clients. He started his career at Weiss, Whitten Stagliano in New York and also did a short stint at TBWA Chiat Day.

He has been honoured by numerous award shows and industry periodicals both in the United States and abroad.

Rick lives in Mill Valley, California, with his wife and three-year-old daughter. When not at the office, he revels in the domestic bliss of his family.

Hunter Hindman, Executive Creative Director and Associate Partner
Hunter started his career at Pyro Brand Development, an experimental offshoot of The Richards Group in Dallas, Texas, and was also a founding member of Tilford:Norman design. He originally joined Goodby, Silverstein & Partners nine years ago, as a young designer, then went to Wieden + Kennedy Amsterdam as a Global Creative Director on Coca-Cola. His work on Coca-Cola garnered global acclaim, most notably for the 'Coke Side of Life' launch and 'Happiness Factory'.

After his 'European vacation' (as Rich Silverstein calls it), he returned to Goodby, Silverstein & Partners in 2007 as a Group Creative Director and Associate Partner. Throughout his career, he has created award-winning work for Nike, HP, Adidas, Converse, Frito-Lay and Hummer among others. Most recently, he has produced the much-lauded campaigns Hotel 626 and Crash the Super Bowl for Frito-Lay's Doritos.

Hunter's work has been recognized in numerous award shows as well as in industry press, both in the United States and abroad. Most notably, he was twice recognized with *Creativity Magazine*'s Campaign of the Year and was named one of the Top 20 creative directors worldwide by the same publication. He was also awarded International Campaign of the Year by *Campaign* magazine and received the prestigious Vision Award from the New York Art Directors Guild.

Hunter lives in Berkeley, California, with his wife, son and rather rowdy English Bull Terrier from the Netherlands, Rommel, named after the Dutch word for 'mess', not the infamous Desert Fox.

CASE STUDY 4

LYNX PRIMAL INSTINCT

The challenge

When Lynx was looking to launch its new 'Instinct' product in Australia it had a fairly specific set of goals:

- to exceed sales figures achieved by the previous year's Lynx product 'Dark Temptation';
- to add an additional 10,000 registered users to the Lynx online database;
- to use rich media, new media and social media to engage and interact with 400,000-plus members of the core target demographic.

Campaign budget

Between A $100,000 and A $200,000.

Target audience

Lynx's core audience is males aged between 14 and 21, who are already familiar with the brand's famous promise: 'Lynx – helps you in the mating game'. The mating game is, of course, as popular as ever with Australia's young males, but the way people play that age-old game has evolved. To connect with them effectively, Lynx's strategy needed to evolve too.

Market research demonstrated that the target demographic were also passionate gamers and extremely social online users:

● 97 per cent of teens aged 12–17 play computer, web, portable or console games; 50 per cent played games 'yesterday'.

● 73 per cent play games on a desktop or a laptop computer.

● More than 75 per cent of the core demographic within Australia are on Myspace.

● Almost 100 per cent of the target audience contact each other each day by way of a social setwork platform.

Action

To launch the new body spray Lynx Instinct, the brand engaged Soap Creative, a leading digital agency in Australia.

The strategy the agency developed was inspired by the name of the new spray, 'Instinct', and set out to bring out the caveman in young males across Australia. On the surface that may not sound like that much of a challenge, until you consider the target species' nomadic nature. Young Aussie males move around a lot online, so Soap decided that the best approach was instead of waiting for the audience to come to them, to take engagement out to the audience. It set about creating a campaign designed to reach out and connect with young men in their natural online habitats: Myspace, Facebook and YouTube, computer games, men's magazine websites and cinemas. Soap took the Lynx Instinct brand out to the places where its target audience naturally congregated online.

The result was an integrated campaign featuring a multi-player online game that proved both popular and addictive. The campaign was supported and amplified across the audience's favoured media channels:

- Interactive media: rich interactive media created impact and awareness. Some banners were also embedded with unique 'game codes' that could be used to advantage when playing the Primal Instinct game.
- Myspace/Bebo: a campaign profile was developed, allowing fans to post comments and receive content such as wallpapers, icons and the Primal Instinct iPhone app.
- iPhone app: Soap developed a Magic 8 Rock app, giving the audience decisive prehistoric wisdom for use in the Primal Instinct game – and in the mating game at large.
- PS3 and Xbox Live: in-game advertising spoke directly to the brand's target market.
- *Ralph* and *FHM*: periodicals for the 'modern caveman' provided promotion and more unique game codes to drive online participation.
- Cinema: a 15-second cinema spot promoted the game experience before movies popular with the target demographic.
- TV commercial: the Lynx Instinct TV commercial drove consumers to the online game at primalinstinct.lynxeffect.com.au. It was seen on TV, the Lynx YouTube channel, the YouTube homepage and Facebook.

Results

Analytics software was used to monitor all game activity, and a dedicated social content manager monitored the online conversations, general social media activity and sentiment surrounding the campaign.

The campaign leveraged the target market's use of online communication channels and social media platforms by integrating with and permeating through key social networks. In addition an online treasure hunt of 'cave babes' was seeded through online and offline media channels, extending the game's reach and engagement, and driving traffic back to the main campaign site.

One set of data that highlights the power of the strategy is the return game play statistics. More than 50 per cent of players returned to play the game more than 25 times and 25 per cent of users returned and played the game more than 100 times. Add to this the average game time of more than 11 minutes and you get a measure of how powerful and engaging the campaign really was.

After the eight-week campaign the key performance indicators (KPIs) identified at the outset had doubled.

Game results

- 689,436 visits;
- 136,000 unique game visits;
- 22,000 registrations;
- an average time spent in-game of 11 minutes 40 seconds.

Myspace and Bebo

- 24,515 unique visitors on Myspace and 18,022 on Bebo;
- 1,715 friends on Myspace and 991 on Bebo;
- 4,777 active native application users within Myspace.

Magazine readership audience

- *FHM* 270,000;
- *Ralph* 321,000.

Interactive rich media

- Takeovers, roadblocks and other interactive ad placements reached more than 11 million unique browsers.
- This resulted in 216,925 unique interactions.

These figures are not inclusive of TV or cinema numbers, or of launch results from the associated iPhone application.

Sales results

- Lynx Instinct body spray is the #2 best-selling body spray in the total male deodorant category (Aztec – National Woolworths scan P0309, measure based on units per store per week).
- Total Lynx shower gel is growing double digits in value at a YTD level +20.5 per cent* driven by Instinct shower gel (*Aztec – National YTD 22/03/09 dollar growth per cent YA).

Lessons

This is a great example of an integrated campaign that spans a variety of digital media effectively to reach the target audience where they choose to hang out online.

Going out to meet and engage with your audience is becoming increasingly important, particularly with teenagers and young adults, who spend a lot of their time in online communities interacting with their friends and peers. By taking the Primal Instinct campaign to them, Lynx managed to engage effectively with its audience out in 'the wild', something which made the 'cave babes' game all the more compelling.

While the campaign was aimed squarely at young men, it certainly garnered wide appeal outside that demographic, as the lead developer found out when he discovered a tribe of mothers chatting about their addiction to the game on online forums.

The Lynx Primal Instinct campaign – tapping in to the 'caveman' instincts of Australia's young men.

Marketers, when you know what it is you want to measure you know you at least have a chance of being successful.

Links to campaign creative

- http://www.lynxeffect.com.au/awardentry/

Credits

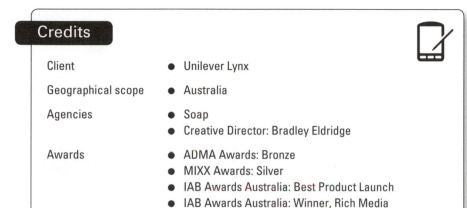

Client	● Unilever Lynx
Geographical scope	● Australia
Agencies	● Soap
	● Creative Director: Bradley Eldridge
Awards	● ADMA Awards: Bronze
	● MIXX Awards: Silver
	● IAB Awards Australia: Best Product Launch
	● IAB Awards Australia: Winner, Rich Media
	● Creative Showcase Australia: Grand Final Winner

Creative biography

Bradley Eldridge

Bradley Eldridge, Creative Director, Soap

Brad Eldridge is a partner and creative director at Soap, one of Australia's leading digital agencies.

At work he helps define the online persona for brands such as 20th Century Fox, 3 Mobile, Cornetto, Magnum, LYNX and Rexona. At home he escapes the corporate world by drawing bottles of beer and playing Milton Bradley's 'Guess Who' with his daughter.

CASE STUDY 5

RAGE AGAINST THE MACHINE FOR CHRISTMAS NUMBER ONE

The challenge

For four years the once coveted Christmas number one spot on the UK singles charts had belonged to Simon Cowell and the winner of his TV talent show *The X Factor*. Since 2005 no other band or artist had been able to stop the *X Factor* winner from topping the UK's once hotly contested festive charts. Music fans Jon Morter and his wife Tracy had had enough… they decided to do something about it.

Campaign budget

£0.00.

Target audience

Music lovers across the UK who, like Jon, were sick of manufactured talent show artists and the massive marketing machine behind them dominating the British music charts.

Action

Jon and Tracy decided to pit the 2009 *X Factor* winner, nice boy Joe McElderry, and his début single 'The Climb', against hard-core Californian rock band Rage Against the Machine and their 1992 single 'Killing In The Name'. They created a Facebook group called 'RAGE AGAINST THE MACHINE FOR CHRISTMAS NO.1' on 22 November 2009, invited their own Facebook friends to join and encouraged them to do the same. Jon kept pressing others to join the group and to promote it to their own online network of contacts using the 'Share' facility on Facebook and Twitter's 'Retweet' option. Dogged persistence paid off.

The group went viral across social media channels and grew explosively. Before long it became a big enough phenomenon to visibly 'rattle' Simon Cowell at an *X Factor* press conference. Rage Against the Machine heard about the campaign and threw their weight behind it in a BBC Radio 5 Live interview alongside Jon, where they performed 'Killing In The Name' complete with expletives, despite the BBC's request that they refrain.

The campaign took on a life of its own, and became headline news across the UK and further afield, crossing the boundaries between digital and traditional media. Big name UK celebrities such as Lenny Henry, Stereophonics, Stephen Fry, Bill Bailey, Phil Jupitus, Prodigy, John Lydon (Sex Pistols), Dave Grohl and Sir Paul McCartney all chimed in with their support, lending even more weight to a juggernaut that had grown at this stage to be every bit as unstoppable as the *X Factor* marketing machine. They were on a collision course.

Results

Described as 'simply one of the biggest shocks in chart history', by BBC News entertainment reporter Colin Paterson, 'Killing In The Name' surged into the Christmas number one spot with more than 500,000 downloads in the week before Christmas, outselling McElderry's cover of the Miley Cyrus ballad 'The Climb' by more than 50,000 copies.

Speaking on the BBC Radio One chart show after the announcement of their success, Zack de la Rocha from Rage Against the Machine applauded what he called an 'incredible organic grassroots campaign', and acknowledged the 'spontaneous action taken by young people throughout the UK to topple this very sterile pop monopoly'.

The campaign also directly raised an impressive £100,000 for the charity Shelter by asking supporters to make a donation. Rage Against the Machine pledged to donate profits from single sales to the same charity, which was a fantastic result for Jon Morter's chosen cause, and offered to put on a free UK concert to celebrate the achievement.

In a purely commercial sense though the real beneficiary here was Sony's Epic music label, which had both McElderry and Rage Against the Machine on its books. Regardless of who ended up clinching the number one spot, Sony was guaranteed a winner.

Following the success of this campaign *X Factor* bosses are allegedly considering shifting the show's schedule to earlier in the year to make sure it doesn't clash with the Christmas charts and elicit a similar social media backlash next year.

Lessons

This campaign, perhaps more than any other over the past few years, demonstrates the incredible power and reach of online social media to influence events in the real world. It also shows what can be achieved by a small, dedicated team, or even an individual, with little or no budget but plenty of drive and determination. It's a classic example of how quickly things can spread across social networks, spilling over into traditional media, and back again as people rush online to check it out having seen, heard or read about it offline.

The neat lines marketers liked to draw between traditional and digital media aren't just blurring, they're fading into oblivion.

The campaign also serves as both a timely wake-up call and a warning to brands about the power of online media to channel public opinion and sentiment. Used in the right way, these emerging channels can be an incredibly effective way to enhance a brand's image, reputation, reach and influence, but the very characteristics that lend social media such huge positive potential can just as easily work the other way. Brands need to think about their social media engagement carefully, and manage it effectively.

The original Facebook group for the campaign peaked at 1.1 million members.

Links to campaign creative

- http://bit.ly/inthename (the original group which peaked at 1.1 million members)

- http://facebook.com/ratm4xmas (the Facebook fan page)

- http://justgiving.com/ratm4xmas (the charity donations page)

For press and internet coverage, Google keywords such as 'rage xmas', 'rage Christmas', 'RATM Cowell', etc.

Credits

Client	• Jon and Tracy Morter
Geographical scope	• United Kingdom
Agencies	• Not applicable
Awards	• The BBC named Jon Morter as one of its men of the year in its 'Faces of the Year' feature for 2009
	• Jon was nominated as 'Digital Marketer of the Year' at the Revolution Awards
	• The campaign was nominated for two JustGiving Charity Awards

CASE STUDY 6

PIZZA HUT IPHONE APPLICATION

The challenge

In an age when young consumers demand everything now, and are eager to find cool new ways to get what they want in faster and ever smarter ways, iconic brand Pizza Hut was looking for a compelling new way to engage with this demanding demographic. They wanted something innovative that would dovetail nicely with people's increasingly hectic and demanding lifestyles, and that would make ordering Pizza Hut quick, easy, convenient and, above all, fun.

While the Pizza Hut brand already leverages a number of online communication channels to engage with its customers, this time it was looking for something little short of revolutionary – something that would take the experience of ordering pizza to a whole new level.

They wanted to create something 'so cool it could feature in an Apple TV commercial'.

Target audience

Today's modern young consumers are busy, constantly on the go and time-starved. They crave products that make their lives a little easier – and they demand that brands deliver.

Pizza Hut's chosen agency, imc², needed a solution that would make Pizza Hut more accessible and convenient – something that could match the demanding lifestyle of its core customer base.

Action

By developing a custom application for Apple's iPhone and iPod Touch, imc² put a whole new way of ordering pizza in the consumers' back pockets. The app allowed people to connect with the brand any time, anywhere. It gave iPhone users their own virtual Pizza Hut, right there on their phone, allowing them to become part of the pizza-making experience.

The app imc² brought the fun part of making a pizza to the consumer, allowing them to effectively 'build their own' pizza on their iPhone or iPod Touch. Using the device's accelerometer and multi-touch interface you could pinch in and out to resize your pizza base, drag and drop toppings, shake your choice of sauce over your chicken wings, drag pasta onto a waiter's tray and more. Once your order was done, you could tap to place it direct with your nearest Pizza Hut restaurant (calculated based on your GPS coordinates if you were on an iPhone).

The application created a consistent, convenient way for consumers to engage with their favourite pizza brand, and the visual ordering experience improved consumer confidence that the order they placed would be understood and fulfilled correctly by their local restaurant, building trust and increasing orders.

Results

Measuring the results of something so ground-breaking can be tricky, because there's no real benchmark against which to compare them. Nothing like this had ever been done before.

Objective 1

Increase brand engagement.

Result

Over 1.2 million downloads in eight months; 100,000 downloads within two weeks of release.

The Pizza Hut iPhone app appeared as the featured icon in the iTunes app store Lifestyle category, consistently ranked in the Top 15 apps in this category and has hit the number one spot in the category. It also featured in the top 25 of all free apps in the App Store, and won several industry awards (see below). The coup de grâce was Apple choosing to feature the app in its iPhone TV commercial and in Apple retail stores across the country.

Objective 2

Increase mobile sales by 20 per cent within six months of launch.

Result

The Pizza Hut iPhone app generated more than US $1 million in sales in three months, which far exceeded the objective in terms of annualized sales.

Brian Niccol, CMO of Pizza Hut, described the application as 'game-changing' and 'an innovation that continues to be talked about'.

'It's an ordering experience unlike anything you've ever experienced. You can build your pizza in an interactive way. You get to engage in the ordering process, which is typically mundane and not all that exciting. Now, we can bring our brand personality to life even in the ordering process using your phone,' he said.

Lessons

While this campaign revolved around an iPhone application, the real lesson here is about innovation. By harnessing digital channels (choosing the right ones for your brand and your market) to meet your customers' needs in new, exciting and engaging ways you can achieve great results. If you make your customers' lives easier, even in a small way (like making it fun, easy and con- venient to order a pizza), they'll thank you by buying more of your products or services, and thinking of you ahead of your competition.

Marketers, if you can, be first to market with something like this, or at least ensure it is vastly superior to the competition if one exists. Pizza Hut clearly took a risk on this investment and it paid off.

Ordering pizza? There's an app for that.

THE PIZZA HUT iPHONE APP

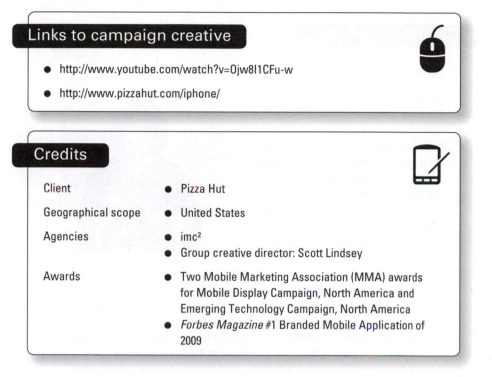

Links to campaign creative

- http://www.youtube.com/watch?v=Ojw8I1CFu-w
- http://www.pizzahut.com/iphone/

Credits

Client	• Pizza Hut
Geographical scope	• United States
Agencies	• imc²
	• Group creative director: Scott Lindsey
Awards	• Two Mobile Marketing Association (MMA) awards for Mobile Display Campaign, North America and Emerging Technology Campaign, North America
	• *Forbes Magazine* #1 Branded Mobile Application of 2009

Creative biography

Scott Lindsey

Scott Lindsey, Group Creative
Director imc².

As a group creative director with imc²,
Scott Lindsey provides high-level vision
and strategy for his team of creative
directors, designers and writers. He sets
the tone and course for approaching
brainstorming, creative development and
execution, always leading with great
enthusiasm. He is ultimately responsible for
energizing his team and pushing them to bring award-winning, best-in-class
creative solutions with measurable results to the table every time.

Scott graduated from the Art Institute International and has over 19 years of
experience providing creative direction for interactive and print design. At imc²,
he has led the creative efforts for many of imc²'s largest clients, including Pizza
Hut, alli and Lean Cuisine. His direction has led to the development of
successful programmes in online media, e-mail marketing, online promotions,
eCommerce and mobile initiatives, with industry-leading results in conversion
and sales.

Before joining imc², Scott contributed to the creative direction at many
leading US creative agencies, including Rapp Collins, Targetbase, Hawkeye
FFWD and Broadcast.com/Yahoo! Scott has worked on high-profile campaigns
for brands such as Gatorade, Toyota, Honda, Sony PlayStation, American
Airlines, Southwest Airlines and Iams.

Scott has an undeniable passion for the interactive space because it is one
of the first and only mediums to allow for the creation of something that has
never been done before. He believes in sky's-the-limit thinking, finding the next
big thing to advance a client's business, owning everything you do, pushing
yourself to the limit and always, always creating.

Scott's words to live by: when you lie down at night, ask yourself, 'Did I
create something awesome today?' If the answer is no, the next question is,
'What's something awesome I can create tomorrow?'

CASE STUDY 7

THE PHOTOGRAPHIC ADVENTURES OF NICK TURPIN

The challenge

Most modern phones have built-in cameras, but few boast an integrated camera with the quality, feel and speed of use of a dedicated digital camera. The Samsung Pixon was one of the first mobile phones to remedy this, with its eight-megapixel on-board camera with a start-up time and feature set to rival a dedicated digital camera. With a Samsung Pixon in their pocket, the tech-savvy photophile need never miss another of those spontaneous moments and priceless memories that crop up so often in everyday life.

Samsung wanted to highlight how the Pixon would put all the capabilities of a dedicated camera in people's pockets 24/7, letting them capture those precious moments in exquisite detail.

Target audience

A 35-year-old single, urban man with a disposable income. He is tech savvy and excited by gadgets. He is into his photography.

Action

The Samsung Pixon's eight megapixels and speed of operation mean that gadget fiends and photophiles never again have to experience that 'wish I had a decent camera on me' feeling. Mobile phone cameras are, by and large, too slow and/or produce poor-quality images. Not so the Samsung Pixon, which behaves like a real camera and captures images in exquisite eight-megapixel detail.

Lean Mean Fighting Machine developed a campaign to showcase just how good the Pixon is for capturing spontaneous moments with the help of professional London-based street photographer Nick Turpin.

So began 'The Photographic Adventures of Nick Turpin': a 28-day journey around the globe documented by Nick using nothing more than a Pixon and his trained photographic eye. Nick, by his own admission, is 'a bit of a control freak', so to make things more interesting the Lean Mean Fighting Machine put his destiny in the hands of thousands of online strangers.

On day one of the campaign Nick took a photo in East Dulwich, London, and posted it to the dedicated website. Online viewers could click anywhere on the photo that interested them. Once they clicked they'd be shown a 'heat-map' style representation of where other people had clicked on the image. The area with the most clicks at the cut-off point dictated Nick's next subject to capture with the Pixon.

Visitors could also cast their 'vote' by clicking on the image in interactive rich media ads strategically placed on other high-traffic web properties, and through a dedicated Facebook application. Once the votes were in Nick had just one hour to choose a destination and make his travel plans before heading off on the next leg of his interactive photo roller coaster.

Viewers could follow Nick's adventures over the 28 days via his Flickr photo-stream, his YouTube video diary and on a geo-tagged Google map showing all of Nick's images – all updated by Nick on his Samsung Pixon phone.

Results

Passive contacts

● 125 million – defined as the number of people known to have been exposed to any of the activity taking place, such as banner placements, but who did not directly interact with the work ie a click, tweet or roll over.

Active contacts

● 450,000 – defined as people known for certain to have directly interacted with the activity, either a YouTube click, tweet, banner click, click on a photo, visit to Flickr, etc.

Lessons

This campaign used digital channels as an effective showcase for the product's key features and benefits. But instead of simply posting content created by the Pixma on product pages on the corporate website, a dedicated product microsite and Samsung-branded social media profiles, Lean Mean Fighting Machine went a step further to create an engaging and compelling experience driven by clever interaction between website visitors and actual content created by the Pixon phone.

As a result the campaign did much more than simply showcase the capabilities of the Pixon, it also created a feeling of involvement and immersion in Nick's 28-day adventure, and by extension in the Samsung Pixon brand.

Crowd sourcing the next step of Nick's journey was the master stroke in this campaign, essentially giving the audience ownership of the campaign and a really strong incentive to return day after day to see what Nick's next assignment was, where he'd decided to go to capture it and of course to cast their vote for the next round.

The Photographic Adventures of Nick Turpin on Flickr.

By harnessing the input of your audience as part of your campaign, learning from them and allowing them to contribute constructively to the direction the campaign takes, you sacrifice an element of creative control, but the level of trust, buy-in and engagement you achieve in return makes it a worthwhile trade.

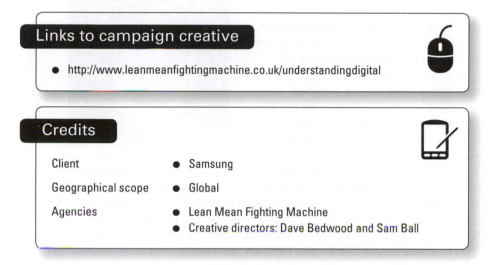

Links to campaign creative

● http://www.leanmeanfightingmachine.co.uk/understandingdigital

Credits

Client	● Samsung
Geographical scope	● Global
Agencies	● Lean Mean Fighting Machine
	● Creative directors: Dave Bedwood and Sam Ball

Creative biographies

Dave Bedwood and Sam Ball

Dave Bedwood, one half of the creative partnership responsible for the Samsung Pixon campaign.

Dave Bedwood has worked with his creative partner Sam Ball since 1995. In 1999, they became one of the first traditional creative teams to get into digital advertising. By 2001 they were Tribal DDB's creative directors. In 2004, they launched (alongside Dave Cox and Tom Bazeley) Lean Mean Fighting Machine. That year they were voted into *Campaign*'s Top Ten Creative Directors as well as *Campaign*'s Faces to Watch.

2005 saw them pick up *Campaign*'s Young Achievers of the Year Award and they were voted by their peers to be the number one creative team in digital advertising. They have picked up numerous industry awards including D&AD, One Show, Cannes, Clio, Creative Circle and the Webbies.

In 2008, they went to Cannes, and with an agency consisting of just 23 people became the first ever UK agency to win 'Interactive Agency of the Year'. In 2009, Dave was the foreman for the D&AD Awards online advertising category, and in 2010 he was the interactive jury chair for the ADC awards.

CASE STUDY 8

TURBOTAX SUPER STATUS

The challenge

TurboTax is the US taxation software for calculating small business and personal tax liability developed by financial software development firm Intuit.

The company wanted to reinforce the mantra that TurboTax is the easiest way for people to secure the biggest tax refund to which they are entitled, guaranteed. They needed a campaign that would engage consumers in an entertaining way, and that would bolster belief in the TurboTax brand, leading more customers to complete their tax returns with TurboTax online.

Target audience

Value seekers who are engaged with online social networks. They are open to doing their taxes with software, do not perceive their taxes to be complex and don't want to pay a lot.

Action

The Super Status campaign was the first ever user-generated content (UGC) campaign where players were invited to solve challenges by posting their answers to their Facebook, Myspace or Twitter status updates in 140 characters or less. By participating, entrants could win high-value prizes simply by writing a clever string of concise text and simultaneously broadcast the TurboTax brand to everyone in their network who viewed their status updates.

The campaign centred around a 'grabbable'/embeddable widget that was produced in multiple sizes, making it easy for users to display the Super Status contest prominently across their online social networking profiles, blogs and other websites, and to view and rise to the latest challenge directly within the widget interface. The campaign involved more than 20 unique challenges which were scheduled to run across the designated US 'tax season'.

At the end of the campaign there was a final contest for the Grand Prize, and a series of 'speed rounds' during the final weeks leading up to the 15 April tax deadline.

Mirroring the TurboTax brand message of ease of completion, the contest provided a low-barrier way to win everything from trips to New York and Los Angeles, to set visits to NBC shows, cash prizes and more.

This was an integrated campaign supported by TV spots, sponsorships, YouTube homepage placements, display ads and search marketing efforts, as well as co-branding and promotional features via the broadcaster NBC.

Results

The Super Status contest was considered a successful experiment in social media. The distribution engine for the widget tracked it as delivering more than 6 million unique impressions. TurboTax judged more than 5,000 entries that were estimated to have garnered around 1 million direct views within players' extended online networks through their status updates based on average friend/follower statistics published in April 2009.

Designed to extend engagement with the brand and support the brand's commitment to innovation online, the campaign prompted media coverage by AdAge, Social Media Today and others as a category-winning example of harnessing social media during the tax season.

Here's how the campaign met its key objectives:

1. Create consumer and media buzz: the nature of the campaign resulted in a lot of discussion and interaction around both the TurboTax brand and the overall campaign, and the individual contests across the targeted social media platforms. It also resulted in positive coverage by high-profile industry commentators such as AdAge, Social Media Today and others, and won an OMMA award.

2. Achieve targeted banner impression reach (200 million impressions): as the contest module lived in widget form as well as on the microsite, the contest was distributed across the web, even finding a home on individuals' own social media profile pages. The result was an estimated 6 million unique impressions (per MixerCast tracking), or three times the pre-campaign goal.

3. Create content engagement (400,000 views/interactions): as entries were status updates, the 5,000 direct entries received resulted in an estimated 1 million direct impressions across players' social networks (per average friend/follower estimates published in April 2009).

Lessons

This campaign's success pivoted on harnessing the burgeoning popularity and disproportionate impact of concise online status updates to engage with social media users and spread brand awareness through their network of contacts. It highlights the power of offering incentives and running contests to promote engagement and encourage propagation through social media.

While the TurboTax example featured high-value prizes, everyone loves to win something, and much smaller contests can generate plenty of social media buzz around your brand and get your name in front of a lot of new people who may not participate themselves, but who are connected to people who do choose to take part.

Marketers, think about the vehicle you use for distribution and engagement. Do you have a widget, and how might you put that particular vehicle to work for your brand? What about an online contest to foster a bit of social media buzz about your brand? What else could get people talking about you positively online?

The TurboTax embeddable widget allowed the contest to travel far and wide, appearing on blogs, social media profiles and websites across the web.

Links to campaign creative

- http://look.daileyads.com/intuit_submissions/superstatus/

An expert view

Simon Priddle, Managing Director, evolvingagency.com

I love this simple idea of challenging the 'status update', and the mechanics of participation are so easy – it's bordering on genius! Simplicity wins, and the message will spread with minimal effort. There is no doubt this campaign has demonstrated a fantastic return, with the number of impressions generated for TurboTax.

I would question the type of relationship you are building: when does a 'brand advocate' become an 'incentivized sales person'?

Is the consumer selling access to their own network for a personal gain or are they making a valuable referral?

Only time will tell the answer, but at its heart this social experiment is brave, innovative and a great foundation for future activity.

Simon Priddle, Managing Director, evolvingagency.com

About Simon

Originally trained as a graphic designer, Simon has been designing and delivering websites since 1997. Simon is now the Managing Director of Evolving, a digital marketing agency. During his career, Simon has been lucky enough to have worked with talented teams and has inspired his clients to innovate. Evolving's 40-strong team has won several awards during his tenure, including two international Webbys in 2010.

Credits

Client	● Turbo Tax/Intuit
Geographical scope	● USA
Agencies	● Dailey
Creative team	● Nick Collier, VP Creative Director, Dailey
	● Jason Simon, VP Director of Digital Services, Dailey
	● Rebecca Arnal, VP Management Supervisor, Dailey
	● Seth Greenberg, Director, National Media & Digital Marketing, Intuit
	● Christine Morrison, Social Media Marketing Manager, Intuit
Awards	● OMMA Finalist, Social Use of Widgets

Creative biographies

Nick Collier and Jason Simon

Nick Collier and Jason Simon started the digital group at Dailey in 2004. Since then, the team has created innovative digital work for Ford, Honda, TurboTax, ConocoPhillips, QuickBooks, Dole Foods, Del Monte Foods and others. In 2009, they received several honours from OMMA, including Best Use of Social Widgets, 2009 Best Rich Media Banner Ad and Best Integrated Digital Campaign (Financial Services). They co-created the first-ever Google/Twitter banner campaign. Their first social media experiment, 'The Tax Rap' for TurboTax, was presented as a Google/YouTube case study and was featured in Entertainment Weekly, Page Six, TMZ and highlighted on a two-minute segment on CNN Money.

Before joining Dailey, Nick was a digital creative director on projects for Logitech, Universal Pictures and Liberty Media, and was on staff at Disney. He attended NYU's Tisch School of the Arts.

Jason Simon, University of Southern California business alumnus, worked in account services for Sapient, leading elements of major web initiatives for Patagonia, Esprit and other major e-tailers.

CASE STUDY 9

THE SPOONFUL

The challenge

Kellogg's wanted to promote its Rice Krispies cereal brand by engaging with US mothers and their children. The brief for this campaign was to help mums to find moments of meaningful connection with their children through the magic of making treats, with the Rice Krispies brand front and centre.

Campaign budget

Incremental/ongoing.

Target audience

Mothers with children under eight years old.

Action

When mums are in 'mum-mode', they're receptive to simple ideas that allow them to make the most of the time they spend with their children. Making Rice Krispies treats is really the easiest thing in the world: most of the fun is finding unique spins on the original recipe and decorating them in different ways.

The Rice Krispies brand is all about helping mums find magic in everyday moments with their kids. For example: listening to the sounds of Snap, Crackle and Pop with their children when they pour milk on the cereal and watching their wide-eyed wonder, or whipping up a batch of Rice Krispies treats and watching their little chefs help to decorate them. The Spoonful newsletter is designed to offer a regular, targeted reminder to mums that there are simple ways to take time out and engage with kids to create enduring memories, even if the world around us never stops spinning.

Results

The Rice Krispies 'The Spoonful' e-newsletter was one prong of the multidisciplinary Childhood is Calling digital campaign. The agency and/or client organization has deemed the results data for this campaign to be proprietary and confidential, and as such have declined to submit the information for inclusion here.

Lessons

E-mail is the granddaddy of online marketing channels, and while it has faced innumerable challenges in terms of relevance, the noise generated by spam and the rise of usurpers to its throne in the shape of social media channels, it still has incredible reach (ask yourself how many people you know with an e-mail address, now compare it to the number you know with, for example, a Facebook account). Used appropriately, e-mail is a tremendously effective way to reach out regularly to a huge pool of customers with targeted, relevant, topical content. E-mail campaigns can help build and maintain awareness of your brand, boost reputation and consumer confidence, keep your customers up to date about new products and services, and offer an effective direct sales channel.

'The Spoonful' is a great example of an e-mail newsletter specifically tailored to engage an audience with a brand. With its primary focus on seasonally relevant activities that mothers can participate in with their children, it engages not just the primary food shopper in the household (mum) but also the primary consumers of the product (children), helping to build next-generation brand awareness and loyalty. The focus on fun activities that parents and children can enjoy together is another plus for this campaign, helping to associate the Rice Krispies brand with positive experiences for everyone involved.

The newsletter design is fun and funky, again ideally tailored to the audience, and ties in well with the website, offering a seamless experience when recipients click through to read the full recipe, browse other recipes or comment on and rate recipes they've already tried.

Any parent with young children already knows how challenging it can be to keep them occupied and engaged. Finding fun, original and productive activities you can do together can be a real challenge, so a campaign like this one, that delivers them direct to a parent's e-mail inbox, was always going to be a winner.

Marketers, don't underestimate the power that e-mail still has to engage your audience and keep your brand front of mind. If you build a solid opt-in e-mail list and deliver regular content that adds real value for your customers e-mail is still one of the most effective marketing channels available, and is typically a fundamental component of a successful integrated marketing strategy.

A sample of 'The Spoonful', Kellogg's e-mail newsletter for the Rice Krispies brand.

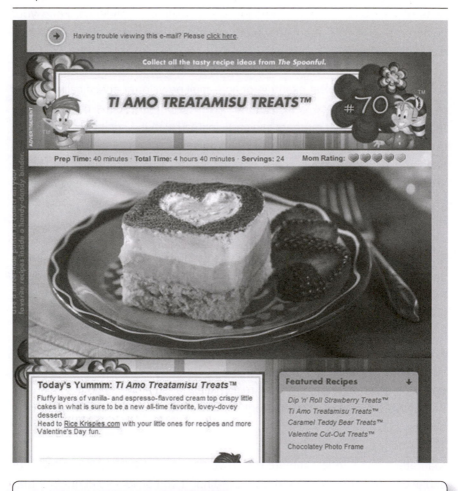

Links to campaign creative

● You can sign up for The Spoonful at www.ricekrispies.com.

An expert view

Matt Butterworth, Strategy Director, Amaze

The Rice Krispies site is excellent, and perfect for mums and children. As a family with three young children we know what it's like to get the kids active in other areas, and the idea of using a brand to bring parents and kids together can only be applauded.

The structure of the site is clear and cohesive, and is genuinely appealing. However, while the content is great, there is room for more social interaction among mums to share ideas and thoughts. While the visual interface is professional the images are a little clichéd and it lacks emotional appeal; uploading and applying user-generated content would make the experience more real and engaging.

Matt Butterworth, Strategy Director, Amaze.

About Matt Butterworth

Matt Butterworth is a Strategy Director working for NMA's top 20 Pan European Digital agency Amaze. An award-winning, motivated, passionate digital entrepreneur and evangelist, Matt has wide international experience of digital planning, strategy and implementation, including residential periods in both Singapore and Kuala Lumpur, and digital consultancy roles in Toronto, San Francisco and Helsinki. He has developed global digital and marketing strategies for clients such as Bridgestone, Barclays, Philips, and Hewlett Packard.

Matt is also an entertaining and engaging industry speaker covering topical issues such as social media, online creative and digital strategy.

Credits

Client	● Kellogg's Rice Krispies
Geographical scope	● USA
Agencies	● Biggs|Gilmore
Creative team	● Associate Creative Director, Wolfgang Hofmann
Awards	● OMMA Finalist: Social Use of Widgets

Creative biography

Wolfgang Hofmann

Wolfgang Hofmann, Associate Creative Director, Biggs|Gilmore.

Wolfgang Hofmann joined Biggs|Gilmore in 2002. In his capacity as Associate Creative Director he focuses on the creative development of digital communication initiatives.

He is a veteran of advertising, and has spent the past decade of his career committed solely to working in the digital space.

'It's exciting to work in a medium that has the potential to make rapid quantum leaps from a technology perspective and has probably the most demanding audience. You can't take anything for granted and you can't make any assumptions. Pair this with result-oriented clients and lean budgets and you have a recipe to rip your hair out. Keeps you humble, keeps you busy, keeps you curious about what's next,' he says.

Before joining the Biggs|Gilmore team Wolfgang was an art director at InterOne (formerly BBDO InterOne) in Munich, Germany. He has worked on national and international accounts including Adidas, Bank of America, BMW, Commerzbank, DuPont, Eaton, MINI, Kellogg's, Kimberly-Clark, Pfizer, Siemens, SAP and Zimmer to name a few.

CASE STUDY 10

IN AN ABSOLUT WORLD

The challenge

The previous brand campaign for Absolut Vodka, where creatives from all over the world interpreted the bottle shape, had been running for 25 years. While the campaign had been incredibly effective, in some markets the brand was starting to experience a 'wear-out' effect. Brand health in the United States in particular was heading in the wrong direction, so Absolut set about initiating an innovative campaign that would rejuvenate its brand image while remaining consistent with the values and preferences of modern consumers. It was also keen to embrace the changes in media due to the impact of the internet.

Target audience

Absolut's primary target with this campaign was the people at the epicentre of the social scene. They are the ones others call on to find out what's going on, and who introduce the coolest new things to their ever-widening circle of friends. These are the social influencers, online and offline!

Action

The aim of 'In an Absolut world' was to spark debate and ask consumers to share their vision of an ideal and more creative world with their peers. On the brand's own website and in other relevant locations online Absolut Vodka stated their vision of an Absolut world through the interpretation of well-known creative individuals who they dubbed 'visionaries'. These visionaries ranged from Kanye West and (at the time) up-and-coming comedian Zach Galifianakis to locally prominent creatives around the world who all got the same brief: 'What's your vision of an Absolut world?'

The second phase of the campaign opened the floor to the creative vision of consumers, encouraging ordinary people to interact with the site and upload their own visions of an Absolut world, and to discuss, comment on and rate the content submitted by their peers. The basic idea was to spark debate both online and offline within different interest areas that matched the target audience profile.

Results

Two principal measures of success were used to asses this campaign: 'buzz' impact and 'viral' impact.

With approximately 500 million editorial impressions during one year the campaign became one of the most discussed digital campaigns, and a huge success in the application of online media. Some of the campaign executions were videos broadcast on YouTube and other video-sharing sites (among others the videos produced by Zach Galifianakis and comedy duo Tim and Eric). With more than 2.5 million views this campaign also constituted a great viral success, and created wider awareness for Absolut Vodka's new brand campaign.

Lessons

While the results of engaging professional creative talent from around the world to kick-start the campaign delivered some truly unique and inspiring works, and an element of 'buzz' around the Absolut brand, things really took off when the creative baton was handed to the web-going public.

'The campaign has been an ongoing experiment, and we have learnt a lot,' commented Ted Persson of Great Works, the agency responsible for the campaign. 'One thing we'd do differently if we were running the same campaign again would be to start realising consumers' visions of an Absolut world earlier. It would have been fun to get the mix between well-known people and unknown/up-and-coming people from the start.'

In an Absolut world, everyone can be a visionary.

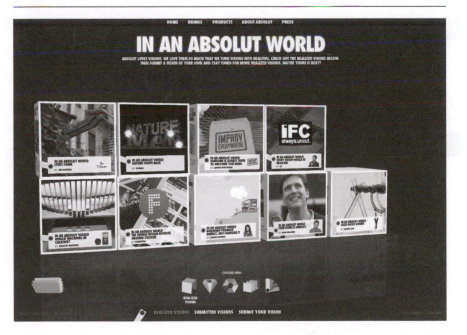

Harnessing the creative vision of online communities can be an incredibly powerful and cost-effective way to generate a lot of unique and attractive brand-related content and to foster online 'buzz' as peers comment on and discuss the stuff they've created on your site and around your brand. People love to express themselves creatively; by offering a channel for them to do so around your brand you can harness the passion of the online community.

Absolut's 'In an Absolut world' campaign is a great example of crowd sourcing creative content in that way, and while the execution in this example smacks very much of a big-brand, high-budget campaign (hiring celebrities for the first phase; utilizing a design-intensive, search unfriendly flash micro-site to showcase content, etc), there's no reason why a smaller business couldn't harness the potential of user-generated content in a similar way using freely available social channels and web technologies to achieve great results on a fraction of the budget.

Links to campaign creative

- http://www.absolut.com/iaaw/
- http://kungsgrillen.se/awards/iaawcampaign/

Credits

Client	● Absolut Vodka
Geographical scope	● Global
Agencies	● Great Works
Creative team	● Creative contact: Ted Persson

CASE STUDY II

WARIO LAND 'SHAKE IT' YOUTUBE SHAKE-UP

The challenge

For the release of the new Wario Land game for its industry-leading Wii console, Nintendo wanted to grab the attention of teenage gamers with something different. The first place teens go to find clips of new video games is YouTube. The challenge was to make the Wario Land preview stand out amidst a sea of competing video game footage.

Campaign budget

US $80,000.

Target audience

Teenage gamers.

Action

The creative team created a YouTube video that appears at first glance to be just another of the many 'sizzle reels' featuring sneak-peeks of upcoming video games.

But there's a twist. As the game footage plays, things take an unexpected turn when Wario's on-screen antics start to affect the entire YouTube screen, trashing the user interface and gradually reducing the page to rubble. Users can then interact with the wreckage of the page, tossing pieces around and even replaying the video in the dislodged player following the carnage.

Results

Success for this campaign was measured in both awareness and total game sales. For the former, the campaign smashed the goal of 12–15 per cent awareness within the target group, reaching an extraordinary 24 per cent according to figures provided by the agency. Game sales fell short of the pre-campaign goal of 350,000 units by the end of 2008, a fact the campaign team attributes to a subdued economy and lower game sales across the industry.

Wario Land 'Shake It' caused quite a stir when it first appeared. It was an interactive first for YouTube, garnered over four million views in just one month and was widely praised across gaming websites and blogs. Two days after launch, Jen Wilson, an interactive producer with Goodby, Silverstein & Partners, overheard an enthusiastic group of kids talking about the page while riding the BART home from work in San Francisco. Within a month or two, copycat interactive ads were appearing all over the web, with similar shaking-and-breaking effects used to disrupt web pages. YouTube told the creative team that they were inundated with calls from advertisers asking 'Why didn't you tell us we could do stuff like that?' The response: 'You never asked.'

Lessons

Internet users are jaded with standard online display advertising – it's more than simple banner blindness, these days many web-savvy youngsters make a conscious effort to avoid run-of-the-mill online ads. Against that backdrop advertisers need to work harder than ever to capture the increasingly fragmented attention of their audience. They need to innovate, to think outside the box… to interact and engage with online communities in truly creative and compelling ways. With the Wario Land 'Shake It' YouTube shake-up Nintendo certainly achieved that.

Marketers, the experience of both agency and advertiser was plain to see here, but why is it that some advertisers always seem to be coming late to the party? Start thinking about the next big thing in digital today – ask your agency to keep an eye on upcoming sites, apps, trends. Actively look for ways to be different, be the first to exploit an opportunity for your brand to stand out, as opposed to being an also-ran. You also need to be mindful of the fickle nature of the digital space – what is leading edge today becomes trailing edge tomorrow.

This market moves much much faster than anything we have ever experienced, and as advertisers you need to match that pace of innovation and change.

Wario shaking up the screen on YouTube.

Links to campaign creative

- http://www.youtube.com/wariolandshakeit2008

Credits

Client	● Nintendo Wii
Geographical scope	● Global
Agencies	● Goodby, Silverstein & Partners
Creative team	● Creative Director: Erik Enberg
	● Art Director: Bryan Houlette
	● Copywriter: Nathaniel Lawlor
Awards	● D&AD Award Online Advertising

CASE STUDY 12

WALL-E

The challenge

Advertising an animated feature comes with its own challenges, but nothing is quite like working on a Disney/Pixar film. The precious qualities that make a Pixar film unique permeate the story, characters and visuals, and demand the utmost respect and care throughout the campaign. Having worked on several Pixar films in the past, the creative team from AvatarLabs understood the challenge ahead of them: they had to find a way to make the heart behind the characters shine through using clean, alluring visuals and a cutting-edge online execution, and they had to do it in a way that would connect with young and old audiences.

Target audience

Families, kids, general movie going audiences.

Action

Respect the brand

Working with a Pixar title was an exciting opportunity for the AvatarLabs team, but one that they needed to approach with care and creativity. This campaign was all about introducing a new line-up of colourful characters, or 'meeting the bots', in a fun and engaging way. As is common with all film campaigns, nothing sells the product quite like video footage. The challenge was to deliver that content in an engaging way without over-designing or over-complicating the presentation, while simultaneously staying faithful to the unique aesthetic of the film.

Be social

The creative team had amazing video content at their disposal, and the (at the time) new-to-the-market Myspace Marquee ad unit seemed like the ideal social platform for sharing that content. But what do you do when the creative content you have blows the spec limitations of your chosen ad placement out of the water?

The team at AvatarLabs decided to leverage their relationship with the Myspace web team, sharing previews of their desired creative execution with their contacts at Myspace, and negotiated special exceptions that allowed them to push well beyond the usual limitations of the Myspace Marquee ad container. They also created a flash-based Myspace profile page for the campaign, offering several 'pods' of rich content and bringing a robust site-like experience directly to the Myspace movie-going community.

Stay ahead of the curve

For 'Treasure Round-up', a game that would form part of the campaign, the creative team wanted to create an activity that was to Flash games what Eve was to robots. They set about researching cutting-edge solutions and discovered the then new Papervision 3D, a Flash plug-in that allows for the manipulation of 3D objects. Although the technology had been used to create small items like navigations in rich media ads, it was virtually untested for a game of this magnitude. With a little trial and error the development department came up with a truly unique online 3D experience for *WALL-E*. The goal of the game is to collect as many objects as you can before *WALL-E*'s power runs out. Mystery objects give *WALL-E* a speed boost, more power or even take some power away. Players could even toggle their point of view (POV) with the space bar, allowing them to fully appreciate the entire spectrum of the 3D gaming environment.

Results

Common web metrics are important in any digital campaign, but for a feature film it all comes down to one thing: opening weekend box office takings. The main goal of any movie campaign is simple: to promote awareness for the film's release and push opening weekend as an event that the movie going public just cannot miss.

According to the AvatarLabs team the *WALL-E* campaign was a lot of fun to work on, but demanded an intense understanding of not only the client's needs, but also the brand's marketing requirements. A thorough understanding of the campaign goals, long-standing relationships with host-site teams and an unwavering desire to push forward with new technologies combined to help the creative team deliver award-winning work that was both simple in the cleanliness of its execution and incredibly complex in the depth of its content.

Bottom line: *WALL-E* went on to become the highest-grossing film on its opening weekend.

Lessons

Successful online promotion is as much about understanding your audience and your campaign goals as any form of advertising has ever been. The scope of options available to the online advertiser is mind-boggling, but having a clear understanding of what's needed to achieve a particular goal, knowing where to find your online audience and how to engage with them effectively when you do is more important than ever. The *WALL-E* campaign also shows how the strategic leverage of existing professional relationships can give your campaign an edge, helping it to stand out in a crowded online marketplace.

The *WALL-E* Myspace profile: an example of knowing your audience and engaging with them where they choose to spend their time online.

Links to campaign creative

- http://avatarclient.com/extranet/awards/2009/wall-e/links.html

Credits

Client	● Disney/Pixar
Geographical scope	● USA
Agencies	● AvatarLabs
Campaign contacts	● Senior Producer: Josh Golsen
	● Creative Director: Laura Primack
	● Executive Creative Director and CEO: Rex Cook
Awards	● 2009 IAC: Best Media Online Campaign
	● 2009 IAC: Best of Show Online Campaign
	● 2009 OMMA Awards: Winner, Homepage Takeover/ Sponsorship
	● 2009 W3 Awards: Gold Award, Online Campaign
	● 2009 W3 Awards: Silver Award, Online Advertising
	● 2009 Davey Awards: Silver Winner, Online Advertising

Creative biographies

Josh Golsen, Laura Primack and Rex Cook

Josh Golsen, Senior Producer, AvatarLabs

Josh is an award-winning producer at AvatarLabs (Encino, California) and has produced digital campaigns for films including *Avatar*, *Star Trek*, *WALL-E* and *Superbad*. Before joining the marketing world in 2007, Josh developed film and television projects for Warner Bros Pictures, New Line Cinema and Artisan Entertainment. He also created and served as Executive Producer on the episodic television series *CollegeTown, USA* for National Lampoon. Josh hails from Oklahoma City and attended Indiana University in Bloomington. He moonlights as a screenplay writer and occasionally graces the stage at a local music venue in Los Angeles.

Laura Primack, Creative Director

Laura is immersed in the rapidly evolving world of online advertising and new media. She graduated from Rhode Island School of Design and has worked at some of Hollywood's most esteemed creative film marketing and design companies in Los Angeles, including DNA Studio, Colony and The Ant Farm. The very first online campaign she worked on at DNA won a Clio, and since then her projects have been honored with the Golden Addy, OMMA, IMAC, DMACS, IAC and Davy Awards. She has been an integral part of AvatarLabs creative department since the company's inception in 2001.

Rex Cook, CEO and Executive Creative Director

Award-winning designer and creative director Rex Cook founded AvatarLabs in 2001. With more than 13 years of experience in creating A-list title treatments, motion graphics and movie trailers, he has managed a wide variety of high-profile projects. He designed the theatrical motion logos for Warner Brothers and Imagine, created trailer graphics for hundreds of major films such as *Harry Potter and the Sorcerer's Stone* and *Independence Day*, and produced the main titles for dozens of films including *Batman Forever* and *Die Hard 3*. As Executive Creative Director of Avatar, Rex uses the technological and creative expertise of his hand-picked team of designers and developers to provide inspired and exceptional solutions for the online and mobile space.

CASE STUDY 13

THE BEST JOB IN THE WORLD

The challenge

Tourism Queensland wanted to increase international awareness of Queensland's islands of the Great Barrier Reef with the goal of transforming this popular day-trip destination into an international tourist's dream holiday. Based on experience, they knew that increasing awareness of the islands of the Great Barrier Reef as an aspirational destination, using a fresh and interesting story, would drive visitor numbers up over the long term.

Campaign budget

A $1,000,000 (however this was extended due to the overwhelming success of the campaign).

Target audience

A specific audience referred to as 'global experience seekers' was the principal target. These people are likely to be self-challengers, youthful travellers with a high level of education who use new technology extensively and have a preference for holiday immersion. They want to get 'in amongst it' and go beyond the major cities and well-established tourist destinations. They were primarily targeted across key markets with a high propensity to visit Australia, namely the UK, Europe, the USA, Japan, Germany, New Zealand, New Caledonia, Ireland, Scandinavia, Singapore, Malaysia, India, China, Taiwan and Korea.

Action

The creative team decided to offer something priceless to entice participation and engagement in this campaign: a prize that would capture the imagination of people all over the world.

In fact, it wasn't a prize at all, it was a job as caretaker of the islands of the Great Barrier Reef.

A clear part of the campaign strategy was to launch as a good news story from the sunny, tropical environs of North Queensland at a time when the northern hemisphere was shrouded in the sullen grey of winter. When this campaign launched the news was full of doom and gloom, and the plan was that this opportunity would break like a breath of balmy fresh air!

The island caretaker role wasn't a campaign gimmick, it was a completely genuine employment opportunity with Tourism Queensland, living on the islands of the Great Barrier Reef and reporting back to the world via online social media. Anyone and everyone was free to apply. Creatively the role was set up specifically to highlight the region and its activities, satisfying the target market's thirst for digital information.

The island caretaker would have specific duties: cleaning the pool, feeding the fish, collecting the mail and, of course, reporting back to the world on their adventures living and working in this unique tropical location. In return for all this hard work the caretaker would earn a generous salary of A $150,000 for six months, with luxury accommodation thrown in. It all seemed too good to be true, but there really was no catch.

Applications for the job opened in January 2009 and would-be caretakers from around the world sent in 60-second videos demonstrating their creativity and skill. From a shortlist of 50 applicants, just 16 were chosen to travel to Queensland in early May 2009 for the final selection process. After a worldwide search involving more than 34,000 applicants, 34-year-old Englishman Ben Southall emerged victorious and was offered the job as Tourism Queensland's Islands Caretaker (the 'Best Job in the World').

Results

'The Best Job in the World' was certainly a resounding success that smashed all expectations and led the team behind it to speculate that 'no single tourism campaign, and perhaps no individual campaign, has ever had such a significant reach or impassioned response, across all media'. That's a bold assertion, but one that is perhaps borne out by the facts.

The success of the campaign was measured in relation to overall reach and its engagement through digital media, but some elements of the campaign, like the passion and creativity with which individuals around the world produced videos, blogs, individual campaigns and so on, really are immeasurable.

Some of the quantifiable measures that help illustrate the phenomenal success of the campaign include the following.

Overall awareness and media coverage

Global news coverage (all media formats), from CNN stories to BBC documentaries, an *Oprah* segment, *Time* magazine article and everything in between. Estimated media coverage is valued at approximately US $368 million (to date and growing). The overall global PR value key performance indicator (KPI) set by Tourism Queensland was US $66 million.

The campaign was ranked eighth on the international list for the world's top 50 public relations stunts of all time by internationally renowned public relations company Taylor Herring.

To date, the campaign has reached an audience of over 3 billion through media coverage.

Direct response

A total of 34,684 one-minute video job applications (KPI 10,000) from 197 countries (web coded as there are officially only 195 UN recognized countries). At least one person from every country in the world applied for the island caretaker position.

More than 475,000 votes were cast for wild card applicants.

A total of 154,437 individuals subscribed to news updates from the dedicated website.

Website stats

There were 8,465,280 visits to the website (KPI 400,000) and 55,002,415 page views with an average time spent of 8.22 minutes.

A Google search for 'best job in the world island' achieves about 148,000,000 listings.

Global reach has been achieved as part of the objectives as illustrated by the international site traffic.

Connection to social media and consumer-generated content at height of campaign

A Google blog search for 'best job in the world' generates 231,355 blogs.

The social media impact could not be measured fully. However, an indication was the fact that Facebook referred 371,126 visits, the highest referring site after Google and Yahoo! Additionally the site has recorded 165,014 exit links to the 'Add This' social bookmarking site.

Social networks have been established by consumers, further illustrating the penetration of the idea (see example on the NING networking site – on this site alone, there are 359 members and 284 videos, representing more than 13 hours of user-generated content).

In terms of consumer-generated content, there are more than 578 hours of campaign-related video across YouTube and similar video-sharing sites.

A 'best job in the world' search on Flickr for pictures gives you a quick 4,486 pictures to choose from.

The team tracked many other samples of video, text and pictorial content. As so much consumer content lies on diverse sites, blogs and in news coverage, it is not possible to accurately quantify it all.

The campaign was helped along by a target audience familiar with social media and eager to share. Individuals were more than happy to fuel the campaign through their habitual use of social networking and sharing sites and regular participation in a wide variety of online communities. The strategic balance of traditional and new media harnessed as part of this campaign proved the ideal vehicle for the message and had an incredibly positive impact on overall results.

Lessons

'The Best Job in the World' is a truly original idea brilliantly executed. It was a phenomenal success and demonstrates just how effective cross-channel, integrated campaigns can be in a world where social media and traditional mass media are inextricably intertwined. The campaign clearly shows that the perceived boundary between digital media and traditional mainstream media really isn't a boundary at all, and that integrated campaigns that harness all appropriate channels to connect with a specific audience can deliver truly outstanding results.

Tension mounts as Tourism Queensland gets down to the final 16 candidates for 'The Best Job in the World'.

Final 16 Applicants

It took the creation of e-mail to change direct mail, the birth of search to disrupt the classified ads market and it took the advent of social media to change public relations.

Marketers, do the results from your PR activity look like this? If not, ask yourself if you are working with the right agency, regardless of whether they are billed as being digital, PR or social media specialsts. This campaign is heralded as ground-breaking in so many ways, but the reality today is that this represents the minimum requirement from what is readily available in the market.

Links to campaign creative

- http://www.sapient.com/en-us/SapientNitro/Work.html#/?project=109
- http://www.islandreefjob.com.au/about-the-best-job

An expert view

Ankur Shah, CEO, Techlightenment

The campaign was hugely successful in both concept and reach. Its impact on traditional media showed the impact that large-scale digital campaigns can have by leveraging the benefits of user generated content and social media. Highly effective usage of Facebook and YouTube clearly helped to drive the phenomenal growth the campaign achieved. The campaign further highlighted the inherently viral elements of self-promotion; utilizing well-motivated users to promote themselves online gains traction across many different mediums and can, if harnessed properly, gain positive brand association. The 'Best Job in the World' was a fantastic demonstration of that.

Ankur Shah, CEO, Techlightenment

About Ankur

Ankur co-founded Techlightenment in 2007 with Gi Fernando, following a successful stint at the Criminal Bar. Techlightenment is a data driven marketing and technology company specializing in social behaviour. Widely regarded as leaders in the space, Techlightenment's most recent product is the first and most powerful advertising management and optimization technology currently available for social advertising. The company also specializes in applications and campaigns for large global brands, counting among its clients brands like Paramount, Betfair and Sport England.

Credits

Client	● Tourism Queensland
Geographical scope	● Global
Agencies	● SapientNitro
Campaign contacts	● Darren McColl
Awards	● Cannes Lions: Cyber Lion, Grand Prix, Interactive Campaigns
	● Cannes Lions: Direct Lion, Grand Prix
	● Cannes Lions: PR Lion, Grand Prix
	● Cannes Lions: PR Lion, Gold, Tourism & Leisure
	● Cannes Lions: PR Lion, Technique, Best Use of the Internet, Digital Media and Social Media
	● Cannes Lions: Direct Lion, Gold, Strategy & Traffic Building
	● Cannes Lions: Direct Lion, Gold, Product & Service Travel, Entertainment and Leisure
	● DMA Echo Awards: Best in Show (Diamond)
	● DMA Echo Awards: Gold
	● DMA Echo Awards: A. Eicoff Broadcast Innovation
	● One Show: Best in Show
	● One Show: Interactive Gold World Medal
	● One Show: Gold, Integrated Branding Campaign

- One Show: Silver, Interactive Digital Media Campaign
- New York Festivals Digital and Interactive: Grand Trophy
- New York Festivals Digital and Interactive: Gold Trophy
- New York Festivals Digital and Interactive: Gold World Medal
- MIXX: Best in Show
- MIXX: Gold, Direct Response and Lead Generation
- MIXX: Gold, International
- MIXX: Gold, Cross Media Integration
- Clio: Gold, Innovative Media

Creative biography

Darren McColl

At SapientNitro Darren McColl is the team's strategic thinker, responsible for helping clients grow their business, by bringing insight to strategy and inspiration to creativity.

With a career spanning more than 20 years, he has worked on the client side and within advertising agencies, large and small. This has given him a great expanse of communication and brand strategy experience.

As a strategist Darren thrives on a challenge and has a natural ability to make the complex become understandable. He has worked across a range of local and global brands including: Virgin Blue, Virgin Megastore, Velocity, McDonald's, Nestlé, Foster's Brewing, Racing Victoria, Ford, Mercedes Benz trucks, Merrill Lynch, Zespri Kiwi Fruit, Yalumba Wines, State Governments of Victoria and Queensland, Mrs Field's Cookies, Tourism Queensland, Stockland, Sanofi Aventis Consumer (Nature's Own, Cenovis, Betadine, etc), Supercheap Auto, Mars Snacks and many more.

He was the project leader and strategist behind 'The Best Job in the World' campaign.

Darren's broad background and skills in communication strategy and marketing make him a versatile beast, and one of Australia's leading brand strategists. He brings to any business sound strategic and insightful thinking, a great understanding in communication and a breadth of experience backed by valuable knowledge.

CASE STUDY 14

STAR TREK

The challenge

When Paramount unleashed its *Star Trek* revamp in 2009, the tag line that accompanied the film was 'Not Your Father's Star Trek'. It's a tag line that perfectly summed up the challenge the creative team faced: how do you take a 40-year-old franchise and make it feel completely fresh, cool and hip for a brand new audience without losing the old audience?

Target audience

Everyone – general movie-going audiences, males, females, families, block-buster fans, science fiction fans, action fans, 'Trekkers', fans of JJ Abrams, etc.

Action

One of the major themes in the film was to make science fiction plausible, to make audiences think about where we could conceivably be 30 years from now. While the creative team couldn't create online placements that were 30 years ahead of their time, they decided to employ bleeding edge technology relatively untested in the online space.

Doing so, and ensuring that the ad placements would work properly when they went live, meant working closely with rich media vendors, websites, the media agency and the film-makers well in advance of the campaign launch. From this approach, two units emerged as the marquee units for the online campaign.

One of the highlights of the campaign was an expandable 728×90 rich media unit that featured a 360-degree revolving recreation of the new Enterprise's bridge that was built using Action Script 3 and Papervision. This was one of the first units to launch with Doubleclick's newly upgraded Action Script 3 enabled advertising platform. The unit featured videos, downloads, a photo gallery and hidden 'Easter eggs' (the ability to put the ship into warp drive by clicking on one of the consoles underneath the main view screen, a first-look exclusive for this ad unit, and the ability to turn on red alert by clicking on the button panel on the right side of the captain's chair).

The unit was crammed with visual and audio effects that came straight from the film. When watching videos on the bridge's view screen, visitors could see many animations provided by Industrial Light and Magic overlaid on the actual video footage, accurately reflecting the look of the view screen from the film itself. The ad also features a larger expansion size of 728×400 to really immerse users in the experience. During the early concepting phases the creative team worked with media agencies and rich ad vendors to make sure that all the sites running the ad unit could deliver the non-standard size.

For the final phase of the campaign the team built a series of home page takeovers that launched on the day of the film's release. The one that had the most impact was a takeover of the MTV home page. Again harnessing the power of Papervision, the effect was amazing – all of the original site's content was sucked into the warp-wake of the Enterprise as it screamed through the page towards the viewer. It was followed by a prominent title and messaging that reminded audiences that the movie was now in theatres.

Other highlights from the campaign included a 'floater' based on the film's opening credits, a takeover on the VH1 home page that showcased the cast of the new film, and several progressive ad placements designed to sell the film's high-octane action.

Results

As mentioned in the *WALL-E* case study, when it comes to measuring the success of feature film campaigns there's a metric that trumps all of the usual analytics data and key performance indicators (KPIs). It's all about the money – specifically what the film grosses on its opening weekend. The pre-release campaign is all about raising the film's profile, maximizing awareness among the film-going public and positioning opening weekend as a must-see event.

With stellar creative, innovative technology and 'cool features', the *Star Trek* campaign 'bridged' the gap between fans of the cult sci-fi series and the general blockbuster movie audience, making science fiction fashionable for all. *Star Trek* went on to take the number one spot at the US box office on its opening weekend, grossing more than any previous film in the franchise, and proving that, thanks in no small part to this online campaign, *Star Trek* could still boldly go where no one had gone before!

Lessons

This big-budget, high-impact campaign shows how far rich media ads have come in a relatively short space of time. It demonstrates how embracing the latest technology, coupled with the innovative application of what's already out there and intelligent placement, can deliver real impact that overcomes the online audience's intrinsic indifference to online ad placements to really grab their attention.

Marketers, if the available budget is there then don't skimp on your banner ads particularly with a product like *Star Trek*, which merits a high-tech, explosive approach. Also don't get too lost in the magic of the moment – outstanding creativity is 'energizing' but it's still important to stick to the principles of objectives and measurement that we rattle on about throughout both books to date. We chose to include this campaign in the book to show what's possible with significant investment into exciting display creative, and on that front it scores very well. However, we can not help but feel that stating your target audience as 'everyone' is missing the point somewhat.

Star Trek's MTV website takeover.

Links to campaign creative

- http://avatarclient.com/extranet/awards/2009/startrek/index.html

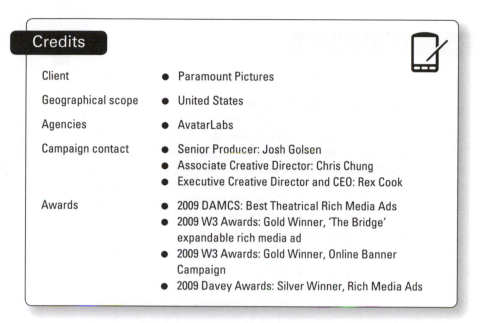

Credits

Client	● Paramount Pictures
Geographical scope	● United States
Agencies	● AvatarLabs
Campaign contact	● Senior Producer: Josh Golsen
	● Associate Creative Director: Chris Chung
	● Executive Creative Director and CEO: Rex Cook
Awards	● 2009 DAMCS: Best Theatrical Rich Media Ads
	● 2009 W3 Awards: Gold Winner, 'The Bridge' expandable rich media ad
	● 2009 W3 Awards: Gold Winner, Online Banner Campaign
	● 2009 Davey Awards: Silver Winner, Rich Media Ads

Creative biographies

Josh Golsen, Chris Chung and Rex Cook

Josh Golsen, Senior Producer, AvatarLabs

Josh is an award-winning producer at AvatarLabs (Encino, California) and has produced digital campaigns for films including *Avatar*, *Star Trek*, *WALL-E* and *Superbad*. Before joining the marketing world in 2007, Josh developed film and television projects for Warner Bros Pictures, New Line Cinema and Artisan Entertainment. He also created and served as Executive Producer on the episodic television series *CollegeTown, USA* for National Lampoon. Josh hails from Oklahoma City and attended Indiana University in Bloomington. He moonlights as a screenplay writer and occasionally graces the stage at a local music venue in Los Angeles.

Chris Chung, Associate Creative Director

Chris has slipped through the settings of Upstate New York, Hong Kong, Taiwan and The University of Michigan. Past co-workers have seen him loitering at Bleu22, Exopolis and Trailer Park. Chris has art directed campaigns for films including *Avatar*, *Sherlock Holmes* and *Star Trek*, and currently holds the position of Associate Creative Director and Asian-Guy-With-Glasses #3 at AvatarLabs in Encino, California. He likes bacon.

Rex Cook, CEO and Executive Creative Director

Award-winning designer and creative director Rex Cook founded AvatarLabs in 2001. With more than 13 years of experience in creating A-list title treatments, motion graphics and movie trailers, he has managed a wide variety of high-profile projects. He designed the theatrical motion logos for Warner Brothers and Imagine, created trailer graphics for hundreds of major films such as *Harry Potter and the Sorcerer's Stone* and *Independence Day*, and produced the main titles for dozens of films including *Batman Forever* and *Die Hard 3*. As Executive Creative Director of Avatar, Rex uses the technological and creative expertise of his hand-picked team of designers and developers to provide inspired and exceptional solutions for the online and mobile space.

CASE STUDY 15

SHADOW NAPPING

The challenge

Foster's asked Play to complement its Shadow Napping TV campaign by utilizing digital channels to improve brand perception and increase sales of Foster's Super Chilled.

Target audience

The principal target audience for the campaign was 18- to 24-year-old males.

Action

Foster's 2008 TV spot saw a gang of Aussie mates raiding the streets of Sydney for shadows in order to keep their pints of Foster's Super Chilled super-chilled. It was a phenomenon that came to be known as 'Shadow Napping'.

While the Aussie Shadow Napping gang was relaxing off set, Play coaxed a challenge from them and, on returning to the UK, the agency orchestrated a nationwide search for a group of British 'mates' who could rise to that challenge. To find likely contenders Play released an online video highlighting the 'Shadow Napping Challenge' across a variety of video-sharing and social media websites. The video gained traction and word spread quickly across the web. The video directed viewers back to the Shadow Napping website, where groups of British 'mates' were invited to register their details and audition to become the 'Shadow Poms'.

At regional auditions across the UK hundreds of groups demonstrated their shadow-napping prowess and highlighted just how far they would go to keep their Foster's Super Chilled super-chilled. Two months on and the self-styled 'Shadow Kings' – five likely lads from Essex who have been mates for more than 10 years – emerged victorious.

Off they went to Sydney, where they would do their damnedest to beat the Aussies at their own game, on their own turf. The team was subjected to a series of challenges ranging from the sublime to the truly ridiculous. Play filmed every step of the group's Aussie adventures and released weekly episodes on the purpose-built Shadow Napping website and on video-sharing platforms. To get visitors even more engaged Play also commissioned an interactive multi-user game called 'Virtual Shadow Napping' that would run as rich media ad units across key high-profile websites for the target demographic.

The ads featured a selection of comical Aussie characters: Doris the old lady, Bruce the karate man, Sheila the lifeguard, Rex the dog and Croc the crocodile. The aim of the game was simple: to 'nap' the unsuspecting characters' shadows as quickly as possible, earning points that could be added to your overall team tally, moving you up the leader board and giving you the chance to win cool prizes. To make things more challenging each individual character had more than 100 cunning defensive moves to thwart the player's shadow-napping endeavours, and the location of the ads kept changing, sending players back to the Shadow Napping website to check a dynamically updated 'hunting map' to find their next virtual shadow napping opportunity. Play also seeded a range of 'cheats' around blogs and forums across the web, each one altering the behaviour of a particular character to make napping their shadow easier.

Results

- Hundreds of groups of mates from all over the UK applied and attended regional auditions across the UK.

- Interactive ads recorded interaction rates 400 per cent in excess of industry benchmarks and average interaction times of more than two minutes.

- Video episodes of the gang's Aussie shadow napping exploits amassed hundreds of thousands of views, and the average user session length on the website was recorded at 10 minutes – well in excess of industry averages.

- An independent brand awareness study conducted by Dynamic Logic concluded that the campaign increased the brand perception for Foster's Super Chilled by 18 per cent.

- The campaign generated high levels of radio and press coverage, particularly across the red tops (popular UK tabloid newspapers), including *The Sun*, *Daily Star* and *The People*.

Lessons

The Foster's Virtual Shadow Napping campaign is a good example of how digital channels can be used to effectively build on and extend the reach of a great idea. Tapping into the natural, historical and sporting rivalry between British and Australian males, and combining it with a common passion (beer), this campaign was always going to resonate with its target audience. How many 18- to 24-year-old British men do you know who could ignore a direct, beer-related challenge from their Australian contemporaries?

Add in a paid-for trip to Sydney, and other prizes for participants in the interactive Shadow Napping online game, and combine with creative execution and you get results that far exceed industry benchmarks and an impressive positive impact on the overall perception of the brand among the target demographic.

A particularly interesting aspect of this campaign is the way its interactive advertising units circumvent the 'banner blindness' that plagues so many online display ad campaigns. By adding an incentive (bankable points that help put the player in contention for a prize) and constantly moving ad units around different websites the game becomes a series of treasure hunts, with people actively seeking out and engaging with the ad units as they move around the web (using the dynamic 'hunting map' on the website as a guide) rather than subconsciously avoiding them. A judicious sprinkling of 'cheats' and shortcuts helps to reinforce the quest-like feel, driving further engagement.

Marketers look for existing deep-seated characteristics that are common to your target demographic and ask how your campaign can leverage those traits to maximize its appeal.

Napping shadows the Aussie way.

Links to campaign creative

- www.playwithus.co.uk/work/fosters/shadowNapping/shadowNapping.html

Credits

Client	• Foster's
Geographical scope	• United Kingdom
Agencies	• Play
Campaign contacts	• Creative Director: Jon Sharpe
Awards	• BIMA: Runner up in Display Advertising

Creative biography

Jon Sharpe

Jon Sharpe, Creative Director, Play.

Jon studied English at King's College London and Education at Cambridge University before beginning his career in interactive advertising in the mid-1990s. After cutting his teeth conceiving campaigns for brands including Virgin and United International Pictures, Jon joined Agency.com in 1999 where he was appointed Digital Marketing Director.

Jon went on to found the London office of Itraffic in 2001 where he spent four years leading a multidisciplinary team and delivering award-winning campaigns for brands including British Airways, Heineken, Wanadoo and NSPCC. In 2005, Jon co-founded Play with M&C Saatchi and former Itraffic colleagues Matt Gorzkowski and Ethan Segal. In the past year, Jon's work has been awarded by bodies as diverse as *Campaign*, *Revolution Magazine*, The IAB and BIMA, and he regularly features as a judge on various industry awards panels.

THE OZOMETER

The challenge

Foster's wanted to use the power of digital interaction to promote the brand's iconic 'no worries' attitude in the UK. The company asked London-based interactive agency Play to help out.

Target audience

The principal target audience was 18- to 24-year-old males.

Action

Play came up with the idea of using people's social media posts as a barometer of the country's 'no worries' attitude, and ranking people, places and celebrities on a custom-built website. Twitter had exploded in the UK, as it had in the United States, and was selected by the Play team as the ideal barometer of real-time sentiments for the digital nation. With the help of a statistical linguist specializing in artificial intelligence, the team crafted a custom built algorithm, dubbed 'The Ozometer', that would analyse tweets (Twitter posts) in real time and give them a 'No Worries' rating based not just on individual words, but also on sentence structure, word pattern, sentiment and context.

'The Ozometer' provided a real-time snapshot of Britain's 'No Worries' attitudes, and fed into the 'No Worries' leader board on the Ozometer website, which displayed the leading 'No Worries' individuals, celebrities and places in the country at any given time. As the online buzz started to grow, the team started to reward tweeting celebrities for their best 'No Worries' tweets, with relevant and carefully thought out prizes that prompted those celebrities to tweet about the campaign and the brand, helping to spread the 'No Worries' message to even more Twitter followers.

To promote and maintain high levels of media coverage, the Play team took the data generated by the Ozometer and used it to compile surveys of the 'No Worries' attitudes of key groups of people likely to prove popular with their target demographic. They released statistics like the top 20 'No Worries' premiership football managers, and the top 'No Worries' *X Factor* contestants which were eagerly lapped up by the media, who created pages of valuable editorial coverage, and even printed the 'No Worries' leader boards.

Results

The campaign really captured the imagination of online consumers and, tellingly, tweeting celebrities with enormous Twitter followings, which helped kick-start viral propagation on Twitter and across other social media sites. The real measure of success for this campaign though was the huge amount of coverage and exposure it gained across both high-profile websites and high-impact offline publications – particularly national tabloid newspapers and men's lifestyle magazines and websites with broad appeal among the target demographic.

Stories about tweeting celebrities and their 'least' or 'most' no-worries atti-tudes were prominent across popular mass media, and the regular 'surveys' of key target groups maintained the momentum so that the brand and the campaign message was reinforced and magnified over time.

All of this online and offline coverage helped to bring the Foster's 'No Worries' message to an estimated 45 million people and promoted a dynamic, ongoing conversation both on- and offline surrounding the 'No Worries' ethos and the Foster's brand. The 'No Worries' studies and celebrity giveaways alone gen-erated an estimated advertising value equivalent of £150,000 in press cover-age, and celebrities tweeting about the campaign to more than 100,000 followers.

Lessons

Harnessing social media trends, such as the burgeoning popularity of Twitter (which was hitting its zenith in terms of explosive growth right about the time this campaign launched) can deliver amazing results and can give skilfully crafted and innovative campaigns potentially massive exposure. The interac-tive nature of social media and the unparallelled reach it has can allow your brand to engage with influencers (celebrity tweeters in this case) in the online community, and through them a huge pool of relevant individuals likely to be interested in what your business or website has to offer.

The team at Play identified an opportunity to create something of value to its target market out of the seemingly random tidal wave of user-generated content created every day by users of Twitter. Together it is just noise, but filtered, analysed and presented in a particular way, suddenly it becomes interesting, engaging and fresh. The campaign also managed to bridge the digital/traditional divide, transcending media boundaries by using Twitter and the Ozometer website as a springboard to generate offline media exposure. That exposure in turn drove more people online, which gave the campaign broader reach and generated even more interest.

Marketers, be wary of promising a campaign will ever go viral. There is nothing more pathetic and job-threatening than the marketer who is so desperate to have a viral hit on their hands they will stoop to extraordinary levels of investment. Instead, learn from this and other case studies such as World Malaria Day. Celebrities will help to ignite a viral campaign but not as much as understanding the personalities and motivations of your audience – the Nokia N97 campaign is a really good example of this. However, there is something soothing and refreshing about a cool brand and cool beer like Foster's to help melt a few barriers in the hunt for engagement – and if that benefit is available to you then use it to its fullest extreme.

What's your 'No Worries' score?

Links to campaign creative

- www.playwithus.co.uk/work/fosters/ozometer/index.html

An expert view

Mike Berry, Digital Marketing Consultant, blogger and trainer

This is an inspired use of social media by an FMCG (fast moving consumer goods) brand. The campaign powerfully chimes with the carefree, free-flowing spirit of Twitter, but goes further to cut through the mass of 'what I had for breakfast' tweets and extract some sense from the streams of chit-chat.

From a PR viewpoint, Foster's and its agency understood the importance of building and then sustaining the momentum. Hence the extension of 'No Worries' to celebrity tweeters and football managers to keep up the level of media engagement and to harness the influence of the celebrities with their large Twitter followings.

The campaign also neatly acts as a bridge between the online and offline worlds; engaging the traditional media including the popular press (which is heavily consumed by this target audience). Print journalists are generally both fascinated by and slightly contemptuous of UGC (user-generated content) in general and Twitter in particular; the 'Ozometer' campaign neatly tapped into this to maximize column inches of coverage.

Overall, the activity was 100 per cent true to the brand and perfectly in tune with the caricature Australian 'No Worries' attitude so famously embodied by Foster's in its UK advertising.

It would have been interesting to extend it into Facebook and YouTube as this audience is also very active on those platforms.

Mike Berry, digital marketing consultant and trainer.

About Mike Berry

Mike Berry is a digital marketing consultant and trainer. In 2002, Mike co-launched SPIRIT, a Central London-based integrated/digital marketing agency with clients including Honda, Marriott, Nestlé, Savoy Group (The Berkeley/Claridge's/The Connaught), Ernst & Young, Bloomberg, Wetherspoon, Sotheby's, Procter & Gamble and Hyundai/Kia. He moved to Jack Morton Worldwide, the inter-public experiential network, as Head of Digital for Europe in 2008. Clients included Nokia, Shell, HP, Toyota and COI (DCSF and The Army).

Mike is the author of *The New Integrated Direct Marketing*, published by Gower, is a Fellow of The Institute of Direct Marketing, for which he lectures regularly (IDM Diploma in Digital Marketing). He is Course Director on the Digital Marketing Workshop for ISBA (Incorporated Society of British Advertisers), Lead Tutor on The Master of Digital Marketing degree offered by Hult International Business School and Econsultancy, and regularly teaches CAM diplomas.

Credits

Client	● Foster's
Geographical scope	● United Kingdom
Agencies	● Play
Campaign contacts	● Creative Partner: Jon Sharpe

Creative biography

Jon Sharpe

Jon Sharpe, Creative Partner, Play.

See page 123 for Jon's full creative biography.

CASE STUDY 17

PLAYING THE CITY

The challenge

The Schirn Kunsthalle in Frankfurt is one of Europe's most renowned art institutions and has hosted more than 180 exhibitions since 1986. Between 20 April and 6 May 2009 the Schirn Kunsthalle invited the citizens of Frankfurt and visitors to the city to participate in and engage with art in public locations across the city centre. No fewer than 23 international artists turned downtown Frankfurt into a living art exhibition with a range of activities and scenarios that ranged from static art installations to street performances and 'guerilla' acts.

The Schirn Kunsthalle team wanted to run a digital campaign in parallel with the event itself. Designed to grab attention, generate awareness and encourage participation in the 'Playing the City' exhibition, the online campaign would need to be innovative and engaging, but without overshadowing the artistic merit of the exhibition itself.

Target audience

Art and culture lovers, residents of and visitors to the city Frankfurt am Main.

Action

To help promote the street art exhibition online, and to encourage people to actually engage and participate in real-world activities on the streets of Frankfurt, the 'Playing the City' campaign used an innovative flash-based website based around the concept of an online interactive board game. Users were able to navigate the site by clicking on sections of a virtual 3D game board depicting locations around Frankfurt, or by clicking on a quirky 'virtual human die' in the bottom left hand corner. Rolling the die caused real people on the page to move around, arranging themselves into patterns representing the number rolled on the die. The user would then be presented with a piece of content representing a section of the virtual game board and a real exhibit on the streets of Frankfurt, thus 'playing' the city. An online calendar allowed people to see all of the events/exhibits at a glance.

Blurring the lines and establishing a tangible connection between the virtual world of the 'Playing the City' website and the real streets of Frankfurt was a fundamental strategy of the campaign. To get the ball rolling, raise public awareness and generate online and offline buzz, the team started the campaign by randomly attaching 'Team-Mates' tags to members of the public at traffic lights around Frankfurt. On discovering the tags later, they were encouraged to go to the 'Playing the City' site and enter a unique code from their particular tag. They were presented with an online video, showing them getting tagged earlier in the day, and inviting them to visit the main exhibition website and to share their experience with their online friends.

As well as the site itself the campaign harnessed a variety of social media tools and online communication media to engage with its audience, generate buzz and promote online conversation around the exhibit. These included an e-mail newsletter, an integrated blog, a YouTube channel, a Twitter account and a Facebook page all spreading the word about 'Playing the City'.

While the campaign was essentially transitory, running only as long as the exhibition itself, there was one element that visitors could keep: a free virtual human die for their iPhone.

Results

Over the three-week period of this highly localized online campaign the website recorded more than 15,000 page views, with visit durations for users from Frankfurt coming in at more than four minutes. During the same period the iPhone dice tool was downloaded more than 6,500 times.

Lessons

Running a digital campaign spanning a very tight time window to drive people to participate in a real-world local event is a very different proposition to harnessing ongoing online marketing techniques to build traffic, reputation and authority for an enduring website. One of the reasons we've included 'Playing the City' in this book is that it demonstrates how digital, when applied creatively, can work at a very local level to engage audiences and enhance participation. It demands a different approach, something a bit different that will capture the audience's imagination instantly.

While a very short, highly localized campaign like this one is never going to match the huge numbers that a sustained digital marketing push can sometimes yield, with an understanding of your audience, the right digital channels and some creative thinking you can create a campaign that delivers genuine value for the target market and, as a result, for your business/client/event.

Marketers, don't be dissuaded from dipping into digital to help your local marketing efforts and to promote transitory events. It's not always about generating big numbers, it's about generating value. What constitutes 'value' in your particular case depends on your circumstances – but do explore the potential of digital channels to deliver.

The Best Digital Marketing Campaigns in the World

Playing the City: harnessing digital innovation to drive local participation.

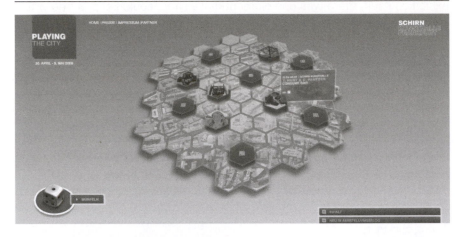

Links to campaign creative

- http://www.neue-digitale.de/projects/schirn_playing_the_city/

Credits

Client	● Schirn Kunsthalle
Geographical scope	● Frankfurt, Germany
Agencies	● Neue Digitale/Razorfish GmbH
Campaign contacts	● Head of Creative: Olaf Czeschner
Awards	● Mobius Awards: Gold
	● London International Advertising Awards: Bronze
	● Annual Multimedia Award: Highlight (Winner)
	● Cresta Award: Gold
	● Deutscher Multimedia Award: Bronze

Creative biography

Olaf Czeschner

As Head of Creative/Chief Creative Officer at Neue Digitale/Razorfish, Olaf
Czeschner guides one of the most successful creative teams in Germany. Olaf
became a managing partner at Neue Digitale in 1999 after working for years as
an independent designer in Germany, the United States and the Netherlands.

During his career Olaf has won more than 100 industry awards and has been
a member of many juries, including Cannes International Advertising Festival,
One Show Interactive, Cresta Grand Jury, ADC New York, New York Festivals
Interactive and ADC Germany. He has a degree in communications design.

CASE STUDY 18

LOST IN SPACE

The challenge

It's hard for IT managers and developers to keep up with changes to their software development projects when they work in geographically and organizationally distributed teams. The flexibility and diversity of distributed project teams has transformed the software development landscape, but the increased freedom and productivity doesn't come without its challenges. Keeping track of who's working on what, when, and of what still needs to be done can be tricky for both managers and developers. They need greater visibility into the team and a better understanding of the process; they need to know who is responsible for what and to easily see where the project is at!

That's what IBM's Rational software technology does and the company needed a campaign to convince IT managers of its merits.

Campaign budget

Circa US $130,000.

Target audience

Size: large enterprises with 1,000 or more employees with software development teams of up to 250 developers (small and medium size teams).

Titles: IT development managers, IT development project leaders, developers, testers, change and release managers.

Action

The Mr Fong – Lost in Space campaign was a multi-faceted demand generation campaign with many different creative elements to communicate the IBM message.

Channels used during the campaign included video e-mails, viral video distribution, a custom-built interactive landing page and various social networking elements like a YouTube channel, Facebook page and Twitter account. These channels combined to communicate one key message: that IBM Rational software offers an agile platform that delivers real-time, in-context collaboration and empowers distributed teams to become more agile and effective.

The campaign started with a video distress call embedded in an e-mail: Mr Fong, the central character of the narrative, was a software developer lost in space, desperately trying to reconnect with his project team. Space was a logical choice to demonstrate how IBM's software can bring people together across great distances. 'We put him up in space because you can't get any further lost than that,' explained Vicki Azarian, creative director at Ogilvy.

From the e-mail, prospects were directed to a specially created interactive landing page, where the story continued to unfold, and they were asked to help Mr Fong reconnect with his team using the on-screen tools. Humorous video highlighted the hilarious results of trying to connect distributed software teams in the wrong way, before Rational software finally helps Mr Fong to do it right.

The original video e-mail was sent out to a permission-based list from IBM's own database, as well as a targeted opt-in list purchased specifically for the campaign. Since the Rational software technology in itself is very much a social tool, Ogilvy set up social media pages for Mr Fong across all the major social networks.

Results

Success for the campaign was measured based on demand generation metrics: e-mail open and click through rates (CTR), landing page visits and offer click throughs. The team also measured brand awareness through PR publications, social media metrics, video metrics and Facebook fan numbers.

The campaign was live for 11 months during which it achieved the following results:

- 17.8 per cent open rate (above benchmark of 12.8 per cent);
- 3.77 per cent CTR (well above benchmark of 0.25 per cent);
- unique visits to landing page: 10,307;
- offer clicks: 1,312;
- registrations: 11.5 per cent of offer clicks (151);
- total video views: 9,848;
- Facebook fan page views: 6,606;
- One pet fish named after Mr Fong!

The original campaign was focused on the United States, but due to its success and widespread appeal it was adapted and rolled out in Brazil, Singapore, Malaysia, Indonesia, Thailand, The Philippines, Vietnam, Spain, the UK, the Czech Republic and Germany.

Lessons

Choosing the right mix of channels to get the message across to your audience is crucial to any digital marketing campaign. Using e-mail as a starting point was a smart move for a company like IBM with a well-established opt-in list of IT managers looking for enterprise-class software solutions – a decision vindicated by the impressive open rates and click through rates the campaign achieved. By directing e-mail traffic to a custom interactive landing page, using a very amiable character in Mr Fong and building a narrative that people could identify with, the campaign took a relatively dry technical subject (software to help with software development) and added a human dimension to it – turning the discovery of a software product into a quest to help Mr Fong in his hour of need.

While it is important to tailor your message to the requirements of your audience, if you can do it in a way that adds a human dimension and weaves a story around your product, service or brand using characters and/or people your audience can identify with, it is much more likely to resonate with them.

Marketers, it's about the pet fish, and the fact that IBM know it was a fish, and that there was only one fish named Mr Fong! The point is, by understanding exactly what it is you want, how you are going to measure it, and then comparing the results with clear objectives, you can quickly identify the success or otherwise of your campaign. We love the fact IBM knew the benchmarks as well as the results. Let's face the facts: this isn't the most interesting subject matter on the planet, but IBM at least proved that it isn't rocket science either.

IBM's multi-faceted Lost in Space campaign introduced an often absent human element to this business-to-business digital campaign.

Links to campaign creative

The campaign is no longer running and unfortunately the live 'landing page' experience is no longer available online. You can view a video overview of the campaign here: http://blip.tv/file/2577477/

An expert view

Nick Suckley, Co-founder agenda21

Most IT communication is bland and it's difficult to engage IT managers at the best of times so it's nice to see campaigns like IBM's Lost in Space standing out with a more human feel to it. The creation of a character who is lost in space is simple and compelling and distributing via e-mail makes sense as IT managers use e-mail as a source of information. The campaign also moved into social media but it felt like a token gesture to me. Interaction rates were strong but overall numbers felt small. However, in this market a small number of sales could yield many licences, so overall, a nice idea well executed.

About Nick Suckley and agenda21

Nick Suckley, Co-founder, agenda21.

Founded in 2005, agenda21 created an opportunity for Nick and co-founders Pete (Robins) and Rhys (Williams), to provide businesses with a 21st-century approach to buying and planning digital media. The integrated digital, search, social and analytics agency enables Nick to pursue his quest for digital excellence, helping companies to harness the economic opportunities that online media presents. Nick is an internet pioneer and successful entrepreneur with more than 10 years' senior experience in working at the forefront of digital advertising in the UK.

Credits

Client	● IBM
Geographical scope	● United States
Agencies	● Ogilvy
Campaign contacts	● Group Creative Director: Victoria Azarian ● Creative Director: Chris Lindau
Awards	● 2009 DMA Awards: International Bronze ECHO

Creative biographies

Vicki Azarian and Chris Lindau

Vicki Azarian, Group Creative
Director, Ogilvy New York.

***Victoria Azarian, Senior Partner, Group
Creative Director, Ogilvy New York***
Victoria Azarian has a long history of
bringing innovation to direct and digital
creative solutions. She embraced digital
applications in the direct marketing space
early on, helping develop one of the first
global viral campaigns to be shortlisted as
a Cannes Cyber Lion for IBM. She has won
nearly every creative award there is to win
in the direct space during her 20-year career. She has been a judge at the Echo
Awards and the John Caples Awards and is a member of the Echo Academy of
Direct Marketing. Among the nearly 30 awards she has taken home are Gold
and Silver Echos, Gold Addy, One Show and Clio shortlists, and Gold Icon
Awards.

Victoria joined Ogilvy five years ago and is responsible for global demand
generation campaigns for IBM that cross all media platforms from direct
response print to digital and traditional mail, all driving successful results for
her clients. She has worked on behalf of global brands in the business-to-
business and consumer space including IBM, Citibank, Bell South, UPS and the
NFL.

Before joining Ogilvy Victoria held senior creative roles at Wunderman/Y&R,
BrannBlau focusing on demand generation and design. Victoria is a graduate of
the Rhode Island School of Design.

Chris Lindau, Creative Director,
Ogilvy New York.

Chris Lindau, Senior Partner, Creative Director, Ogilvy New York
Over the past 20 years Chris has created advertising for everything from finance to fashion to cars to computers. Beginning as a copywriter in NYC, Chris worked at Lowe and Partners, as well as Kirshenbaum and Bond, before landing at Ammirati & Puris. While at Ammirati, Chris helped launch several products for Compaq Computer, applying consumer sensibility to what had previously been a technical marketplace. Bitten by the technology bug, Chris then headed to FCB in San Francisco. There he helped launch Excite.com and Amazon.com, being among the first to use splashy TV efforts to get attention for these then-tiny companies.

For Palm Computing's inaugural television effort, he showed how a PDA could introduce strangers on a train by 'beaming' contact information. Moving to Citron Haligman Bedecarre (now AKQA) for the height of the internet boom, Chris continued promoting internet companies – including one founded by his wife – using pioneering tactics such as planting models in first class using the latest laptop to interactive billboards beaming applications and invitations to Palm users. At Publicis and Hal Riney, Chris created demand for HP printers and inks by opening a temporary art gallery where consumers could print and mount their photos. The results and the stories around them became the backbone of an innovative half-hour programme on how to print – an 'educational informercial'.

Chris's work has earned recognition from industry publications and shows such as Communication Arts, The One Show, Adweek, ECHO, The SF Show and Graphis. He has been with Ogilvy for five years now, where he applies his expertise to the IBM account.

CASE STUDY 19

ONLINE AS IT HAPPENS

The challenge

Mobile market leader Nokia needed to capture the imagination of the burgeoning smartphone market with the launch of the new Nokia N97. The challenge for the digital campaign was to find a way to help Nokia users understand and play with the new tools available to them through the N97, and introduce them to the wonders of being 'Online as it happens'.

Campaign budget

Circa €200,000.

Target audience

The primary target market for the new smartphone consisted of modern early adopters and technology-focused consumers who would be attracted to the tools available on the N97. Those keen to play, who are well informed about technology and gadgets; heavy internet and computer users; those who are very positive towards mobile entertainment in general (music, video games and imaging); those who are prepared to pay high prices for their mobile devices, really use all the available technology and tools and replace it most frequently.

Action

The launch of the Nokia N97 marked the birth of the live home screen. With this feature, downloaded widgets from Nokia's 'Ovi Store' update in real time whenever something changes, and with the Nokia N97 in your pocket you're always 'online as it happens'.

To highlight this 'always connected' aspect of the N97 the creative team developed a campaign that focused on widgets users could personally customize to deliver real-time information. In other words, the campaign would let people create their own customized widgets for their blogs, websites and social media profiles.

On the campaign microsite the user could decide what they wanted their widget to do: for example they could select a widget to display updates on a 'hot' topic, measure the frequency of the search term they use, or compare two words, names or other items on their favourite sites. They then selected the source site the widget would gather the information from and chose how they wanted the widget to visualize the data. If the user was interested in staying up to date with current events, for example, they might choose CNN. com or news.bbc.co.uk as their source sites.

The resulting widgets could be embedded anywhere on the web, but that wasn't all – every widget could also be submitted into a global competition for the chance to be developed into a real mobile widget for Nokia devices.

With more than 30,000 entries, there were plenty to choose from.

So in summary, users created their own online widgets and shared them online through blogs, websites and social media, and the best widgets were transformed into mobile widgets for all Nokia devices and made available on the company's Ovi Store where everybody could download them for free.

Results

The campaign had generated more than 30,000 entries at the time of writing, and was still running, so final figures and metrics were unavailable.

Lessons

People love creating their own stuff online… and they love to share. Widgets allow them to do both.

Marketers, we are starting to see a theme throughout these studies. Engagement, co-creation and if it works globally then do that too. Nokia is really up against it these days. Imagine having to compete with new kids like iPhone and Android and yet it didn't lose sight of its objectives and was able to appeal to its target audience in a meaningful and human way. What do early adopters and heavy tech heads like? Bragging rights!

What better bragging rights than seeing your widget, your creation, being downloaded and adopted by others including the mighty Nokia? And once they understood they were up against the rest of the planet it surely must have got them excited and engaged too. The agency clearly understood the personality and the motivation of the target audience and applied it in a practical way without being gimmicky and cheesy. Good work.

Get the latest… whatever… online, as it happens with Nokia.

Credits

Client	● Nokia
Geographical scope	● Global
Agencies	● Farfar (Stockholm)
Campaign contacts	● Erik Norin

Creative biography

Erik Norin

Erik Norin is a multi-award-winning creative who has worked at Farfar for the past eight years. Before that he worked with Houdini in Stockholm and Dennis Interactive in New York. He has been a member of numerous juries, held workshops in Cannes, given lectures and is responsible for the Farfar Academy (www.farfaracademy.com).

CASE STUDY 20

THE EPHEMERAL MUSEUM

The challenge

The challenge was simple: to launch Pampero Rum in Portugal – a country where rum was seen primarily as a drink for 'old and boring people'. The challenge was to make Pampero 'cool'.

Campaign budget

€30,000.

Target audience

For this campaign the creative team decided to focus on the social tribe known locally as 'Indie'. Why? Because they are the opinion leaders and trendsetters. They dictate what is cool and what's not. If they say Pampero is cool, everybody else agrees with them. Job done.

Traditional advertising simply doesn't cut it with this tribe; a heady combination of digital and art unequivocally does.

Action

Using Pampero Fundación, a foundation created by the brand to support alternative artists, the campaign created the world's first 'ephemeral museum' to highlight the wonderful street art of Lisbon before the local authority could implement a plan to 'clean it up'.

The team started by identifying the best pieces of street art in Lisbon's Bairro Alto district. They then created a central website with details of the art, a map and a downloadable MP3 audio guide – everything you'd need to hit the streets with your MP3 player and experience some of the most outstanding alternative art in the city… and all for free. Social media channels were also harnessed to foster conversation and buzz around the whole 'ephemeral museum' concept.

Results

With an annual budget of only €30,000 the campaign generated brand visibility with an estimated value of more than €940,000, and counting.

According to Millward Brown (Brand Image Tracker), in a few short months Pampero hit sales expectation for the entire year, doubled its trial percentage and tripled its 'Top of Mind' percentage. Pampero matched its leading competitor in sales and in brand awareness level, which is truly remarkable considering that the competitor has been in the market for 15 years.

In practically no time, Lisbon's Ephemeral Museum had way more visitors than any museum in the area, and soon afterwards two new ephemeral galleries were opened in Lisbon.

The concept generated media coverage from around the globe and was written about in hundreds of articles across a wide variety of media, including several leading tourism guides.

Building on the success of this campaign Pampero is now working to open similar street art galleries in Italy, Spain, France and the UK.

Lessons

The best digital campaigns often involve simple ideas, elegantly executed. The Ephemeral Museum is a prime example of that. The team took one of the brand's key values – to support upcoming alternative artists – and combined it with current events (the local authority's plan to 'clean up' street art in the Bairro Alto district of Lisbon), packaging it in a way that would engage an online audience. By replicating the audio guide experience found in contemporary museums the world over, it made the street art of Lisbon accessible to a mass audience.

In a complicated world, web users identify with simple, well-executed ideas that can add value without adding to the complexity of their already hectic lives.

Marketers, don't let the size of your budget dissuade you from exploring a big idea. This campaign *sounds* expensive – museums, street art, civic issues, downloadable stuff and so on. The key to this campaign was Leo Burnett's decision to focus on the catalyst – as Seth Godin would call them, 'the sneezers', those unbearably cool and prophetic types who seem to lead where others follow. These sneezers can often be more savvy about marketing per se and sufficiently sceptical about the usual attempts by marketers to ingratiate themselves towards what is 'hot' and what is not.

Health warning – remember to get it right, make it worthwhile and keep it real. While it is great to attract the attention of this type of target it needs to be managed carefully so it doesn't backfire and put you in a position of ridicule and contempt. Leo Burnett got the balance right – nice to see that the same agency that broke the mould with the Jolly Green Giant back in the 1920s is still cranking its stuff almost 100 years later.

Turning the streets of Lisbon into an art gallery: the world's first ephemeral museum.

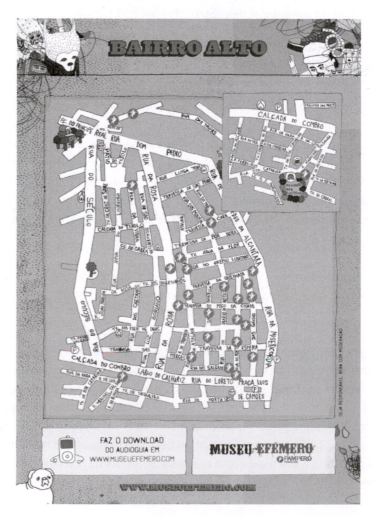

Links to campaign creative

- http://museuefemero.com
- http://museuefemero.com/awards/

Credits

Client	● Pampero Rum
Geographical scope	● Portugal
Agencies	● Leo Burnett, Lisbon
Campaign contacts	● Copywriter: Juan Christmann
Awards	● Cannes 2009: Gold Lion – PR, Silver Lion – Media, Bronze Lion – Promo
	● Eurobest: Grand Prix – Media
	● D&AD 2009: IN BOOK – Integrated Campaign
	● One Show 2009: Merit – Integrated Campaign
	● Cresta Awards: Grand Prix

Creative biography

Juan Christmann

Juan Christmann, Copywriter,
Leo Burnett, Lisbon.

Juan started his career with DDB
Argentina, and two years later accepted an
offer to work at Ogilvy Argentina, where he
stayed for a year and a half, honing his
creative talent on a wide variety of
campaigns. In 2007, he was offered a
position with Leo Burnett in Lisbon,
Portugal, where he began work on the Pampero account, among others. While
Juan was our primary point of contact with Leo Burnett, Lisbon, for the
Ephemeral Museum campaign, he was at pains to point out that it was a
collaborative effort, and that practically everyone in the agency was involved in
this extraordinary project in one way or another.

CASE STUDY 21

PEPSI MAKES YOUR DAY

The challenge

In Turkey, Pepsi started its summer campaign determined to boost market share by increasing sales of its multi-serve products and family packs. Previous Turkish campaigns had successfully driven sales of single-serve units, largely through the selective targeting of young people, particularly using mobile 'text-to-win'-style promotions. This time Pepsi wanted to focus on family-size products, and that meant reaching out to the principal shopper in the household, which in Turkey meant housewives, a group less willing and eager to engage through mobile channels than the youngsters Pepsi had targeted so successfully in the past.

Campaign budget

Not disclosed, but included 27.2 million free airtime units (FAUs) to give away as part of the campaign.

Target audience

The focus of this campaign was on Turkish housewives, typically the principal shoppers in the household.

Action

Previous Pepsi promotions with a younger target audience had proved that the chance of winning free mobile 'airtime' on promotional packs could be a very successful strategy. For this campaign the team decided to offer 10 FAUs as an 'instant win' for purchasing Pepsi's family-size bottles. In addition to the free calls on offer via promotional packs, cash prizes were offered – a particularly alluring incentive given the economic backdrop against which the campaign would play out.

To really hit the mark though, the campaign would need endorsement from an opinion leader – someone who could convince Turkish housewives of the merits of the campaign, and show them how the 'text-to-win' mobile promotion model worked. The campaign needed to be attractive, compelling and incredibly easy if housewives were going to participate in it. Research suggested the most trustworthy celebrity in Turkey was Seda Sayan, widely regarded as Turkey's Oprah Winfrey. She was selected by the Pepsi team as the spokesperson for the campaign. On TV ads and her morning shows, she demonstrated how to SMS and participate in the Pepsi promotion every day.

But despite the celebrity endorsement and TV promotion, the campaign still needed to genuinely motivate housewives to engage and, crucially, to share the message with other people. And that's where the innovative 'promo tone' comes into play. The 'promo tone' is a promotional ringback tone (RBT) that instantly credits the 'owner' with free airtime when another person calls them and listens to the message. The 'Pepsi Makes Your Day' campaign was the first time this kind of promotion had been used in Turkey.

Here is how it worked. Participants bought a family pack of Pepsi and found the unique promotional code on the underside of the lid. They would text the code to a number on the pack and receive an interactive voice response (IVR) call with a message from Seda Sayan congratulating them for winning 10 FAUs. The message also informed them that a special Pepsi promo tone had been assigned to their mobile for the next 24 hours, winning them extra credits whenever people called their phone and listened to the message.

Whenever anyone called the participants during that 24 hours they would hear the Pepsi RBT and a message informing them that their friend had earned free mobile airtime units with Pepsi, and that they could do the same by simply texting in the code from special promotional family packs of Pepsi. 'Drink Pepsi, text the code and you can win too! Pepsi makes your day!', it concluded.

Consumers were free to opt out of the messages at any time. However, consumer engagement was so high that the overall opt-out rate of the Pepsi promo tone was just 1.3 per cent. Both the IVR recordings and the promo tones were changed frequently throughout the campaign, keeping them fresh, maintaining the engagement and fostering word-of-mouth propagation of the Pepsi promotion. On average, four different people called the participants during the day, all of them exposed to different promo tones, amplifying the viral effect of the promotion.

The campaign used several other mobile marketing tools, including wap banners, mobile games, wallpapers and Pepsi ringtones. Turkcell's recently launched 'Click-to-Win' mobile application was also tested for the first time during the campaign.

Results

A total of 3.3 million unique individuals participated in the campaign, almost doubling previous promotions. Four out of every five participants were first-time participants who hadn't entered any Pepsi promotion in the past.

On average, 225,000 SMS messages were received each day. Overall participation was in excess of 16.2 million messages.

A total of 5.7 million people called participants with the Pepsi promo tone during the campaign, resulting in the Pepsi jingle and message being listened to more than 20 million times. IVR calls created the desired effect: 82 per cent of participants didn't hang up and listened to the entire call.

The campaign outperformed all previous Pepsi promotions and overreached sales targets. For the first time 63 per cent of sales came from multi-serve packs and Pepsi's market share in multi-serves increased by 17 per cent.

The total cumulative market share of Pepsi increased by 5 per cent.

Lessons

With any campaign it's crucial to tailor your offering to both the needs of your target audience and the environment in which they find themselves at the time. That's exactly what the creative team did here, using a combination of free mobile phone talktime and cash prizes as an incentive for people to engage with the campaign, and selecting the mobile phone as a practically ubiquitous vehicle to reach out and connect with their selected market. The success of the campaign shows the potential of a creative mobile campaign effectively executed.

A particularly interesting aspect of this campaign is the way the team encouraged the target market to engage through a digital channel that they had previously been unfamiliar or uncomfortable with. Using a celebrity advocate to guide and encourage them, the campaign leveraged traditional media to persuade housewives to embrace the text-to-win promotional model, driving them to engage through its reach and creating a fertile foundation for the next text-to-win promotion the team runs.

Marketers, lest we forget this is all about return on investment (ROI). The agency should be applauded for demonstrating their clear understanding of

ROI and how it could be applied across a relatively new channel 'viral mobile'. Sadly, we don't know what 5 per cent cumulative market share looks like in terms of Turkish lira but it must be a whole lot of refreshment for both the audience and client alike. However, even though they won't tell us what this means in financial terms (get a life Pepsi), one key lesson here is the importance of what you actually do measure. In this instance the agency has provided some really good metrics and you can tell this didn't happen by accident. Clearly the agency knew the objectives well in advance and set out what they were going to count and what constituted success.

The 'Pepsi Makes Your Day' campaign took mobile marketing to the Turkish housewife with the help of high-profile celebrity host Seda Sayan.

Credits

Client	● Pepsi Bottling Group Turkey
Geographical scope	● Turkey
Agencies	● Rabarba Digital Ad Agency
Campaign contacts	● Oguz Savasan
Awards	● MMA Awards 2009: Industry Award for Innovation: Creativity
	● MMA Awards 2009: Best Multi-Channel Mobile Campaign

Creative biography

Oguz Savasan

Oguz Savasan is a partner in Rabarba Digital Ad Agency in Istanbul. Born in 1970, he graduated from Robert College, the American High School in Istanbul and went on to study mechanical engineering at Bosphorus University, Istanbul. In 1994, he received his MBA in strategy from City University London Business School. He has worked as a brand manager in Unilever, and a marketing and sales manager with the Eczacibasi Group – a Turkish conglomerate with operations in FMCG (fast moving consumer goods), healthcare and building materials. In 2000, Oguz joined Young & Rubicam, Istanbul, as Head of Strategy, where he met Serdar Erener, now his business partner at Rabarba. His clients included local giants such as Turkcell, Arcelik and Garanti Bank, as well as Y&R's global clients including Colgate, Danone and Kraft Foods. In 2004, he set up Alametifarika, an independent agency in Istanbul, with his management colleagues from Y&R. Between 2004 and 2007 his work earned him four Gold Effies and two Silver Effies. In August 2007, Oguz established digital advertising agency Rabarba with Erener, and together they have grown the business to became one of the most award-winning agencies in Turkey.

CASE STUDY 22

l2 CAMS CREATE YOUR RAINBOW

The challenge

To use digital channels to both promote the TV programme covering Radiohead's Japanese tour, but also to increase brand awareness for major Japanese pay-TV channel, WOWOW.

Target audience

Japanese TV viewers (although not necessarily WOWOW subscribers) with an interest in foreign music in general and Radiohead in particular.

Action

The team created a website to act as the online hub for the campaign. Content on the site was developed to promote the Radiohead live event TV programme, but also incorporated interactive features that would involve and engage the audience, building a feeling of involvement and community.

A month before the programme was to be broadcast, unedited footage from 12 cameras of the band playing the concert was made available on the web. Users could switch between the cameras in real time, editing the feeds to produce their own unique viewing experience over the internet. Each user's activity was recorded as a series of colour-coded bars that coincided with their camera choices, and the resulting 'rainbow' was shared on the web. Users could compare their rainbow to those of their peers, and post their own 'rainbows' as widgets to their blogs, social media profiles and websites.

All the rainbows created during the campaign were accumulated as an archive of cascading rainbows that could be viewed online. The whole rainbow concept tied in perfectly with the title of Radiohead's latest album 'In Rainbows'.

Results

No advertising was purchased as part of the campaign, but the website was featured by many prominent blogs and news websites both inside and outside Japan. The highest level of activity occurred immediately after the event, and the widespread coverage enhanced the brand image of both the artists and the broadcasting company.

Lessons

Co-creation is becoming a much-used trend and opportunity in the world of marketing. Digital has the power to accentuate co-creation to levels unexperienced by other media.

Marketers, consider the possibility of your customers playing around with your brand. Is it so bad to be parodied in viral marketing? What is worse than being talked about? Exactly.

Examine ways in which your target audience can have some real say and some real influence with what goes on within and around your brand. Walkers Crisps managed to get their customers to devise new flavours – a strategy now being adopted by nearly every pizza place I gorge within; Dell allowed customers to design their own PC, and so on. What can you do that will pass the controls over to your audience and let them drive for a bit?

Thousands of user-generated rainbows scroll up a dedicated page on the WOWOW website.

Links to campaign creative

- http://www.wowow.co.jp/music/radiohead/special/
- http://awards.dandad.org/2009/categories/onln/
  online-advertising/19551/12-cams-create-your-rainbow

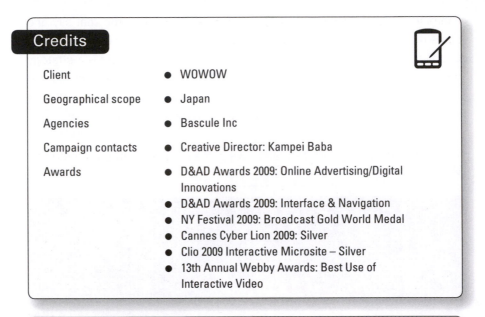

Credits

Client	• WOWOW
Geographical scope	• Japan
Agencies	• Bascule Inc
Campaign contacts	• Creative Director: Kampei Baba
Awards	• D&AD Awards 2009: Online Advertising/Digital Innovations
	• D&AD Awards 2009: Interface & Navigation
	• NY Festival 2009: Broadcast Gold World Medal
	• Cannes Cyber Lion 2009: Silver
	• Clio 2009 Interactive Microsite – Silver
	• 13th Annual Webby Awards: Best Use of Interactive Video

Creative biography

Kampei Baba

Kampei Baba was born in 1976. He has been a member of the team at Bascule since 2002. Today he is primarily responsible for planning and developing flash-based interactive content.

CASE STUDY 23

WORLD MALARIA DAY TWITTER WAR

The challenge

Malaria No More, a not-for-profit non-governmental organization dedicated to ending malaria deaths in Africa, wanted to raise the profile of World Malaria Day, increase awareness of the malaria problem in Africa and promote Malaria No More's mission to end malaria deaths. Once Ashton Kutcher challenged CNN, the goal was to leverage an experiment in new media versus old media, with the net result for social good.

Campaign budget

US $0.00.

Target audience

Twitter users and anyone with a pulse to social media and social good.

Action

For World Malaria Day, Malaria No More and high-profile Twitter celebrity Ashton Kutcher partnered to raise awareness on Twitter. Ashton decided to take the partnership a step further by daring CNN's breaking news Twitter feed to race him to one million followers on the micro-blogging platform. Ashton pledged to donate 10,000 mosquito nets to Malaria No More if he got there first – which he did – and the rest is history.

CNN matched his net pledge, and the 'twitterati,' including Oprah and Ryan Seacrest plus individual 'twitterers' around the world, donated nets through Malaria No More as well.

The 89,724 life-saving bed nets donated through the campaign have been distributed to African families in Senegal.

Results

- Awareness about malaria spread exponentially on Twitter as millions of twitterers learned about malaria and what they could do to help.

- A 10,000 per cent increase in @malarianomore followers on Twitter to stay informed of progress about malaria directly as Ashton and millions more spread the word around the world by re-tweeting.

- A surge of traffic to MalariaNoMore.org, generating more visitors in April than the previous 12 months combined, by individuals learning about the disease and the global effort.

- An outpouring of support on the Malaria No More web petition to President Obama and Congress to urge support of malaria control funding.

- Millions of media impressions, bringing the message of malaria awareness to a much broader audience.

- Most re-tweeted message on Twitter for 25 April 2009 was: 'Every 30 seconds a child dies from malaria. Nets save lives. Support World Malaria Day = www.malarianomore.org'.

- A mass awareness effort on Twitter that made World Malaria Day a top 10 most-Tweeted phrase on 25 April.

- Small dollar donations from individuals on Twitter effectively matched Ashton's pledge (of 10,000 nets), and with help from the 'twitterati' over US $500,000 was raised on Twitter alone.

- As a result of the enormous effort, backed by celebrity Twitter users, including Anderson Cooper (@AndersonCooper), Sean 'Diddy' Combs (@iamdiddy), Oprah Winfrey (@Oprah), Ryan Seacrest (@RyanSeacrest) and thousands of non-celeb Twitterers, 89,724 life-saving mosquito nets were distributed in Africa from January 2010.

- Individual mosquito net donations came from people spanning 42 countries, moved to do their part in the global effort to end malaria deaths.

Some high-profile celebrity tweets

Ashton Kutcher (@aplusk): I'm calling to have a check made out for $100,000 to the Malaria No More Fund

Demi Moore (@mrskutcher): Many of you have been asking so here is the info on Malaria – http://www.malarianomore.org and you can follow @malarianomore Thanks so much

Mark Wahlberg (@Mark_Wahlberg): Every 30 seconds a child dies from malaria. Nets save lives. Support World Malaria Day = https://give.malarianomore.org (via @aplusk)

Oprah (@oprah) @mrskutcher count me in for 10 thousand nets

Ryan Seacrest (@RyanSeacrest): Ashton got me in for 10,000 nets today... larry king is in too. Happy friday

Lessons

You read a lot about the potential of social media to create a groundswell of support around a cause, a product or a brand. But capturing the imagination of social online communities and building the momentum to create a powerful movement that embraces and endorses your original goals is difficult. You need to be creative, you need to be involved in the right online communities, you need to time things right and you need to engage with those communities in a way that does more than pique their curiosity. You need their sustained attention.

With social media in particular that attention is highly fragmented. To break through the noise you have to do something different – something that stands out. Something like getting a high-profile member of the online community you're working with to challenge an iconic brand to a duel.

Ashton Kutcher's challenge to CNN lifted Malaria No More's awareness campaign to another level, catapulting its reach and influence into the stratosphere, and capturing the imagination of traditional media, which pushed the campaign's reach even further. Of course, getting A-list celebrities on board as advocates helps, but a great idea – especially one focused on a worthwhile cause – that really captures people's imagination can spread quickly online without celebrity influence. On Twitter in particular, if you can initiate that groundswell of support from the masses, and get your topic trending, you may well find some big names weighing in with support.

Marketers, aside from the worthiness and influence of this campaign, consider the global elements. Digital lifts the geographical restrictions that often exist. If your campaign is not sensitive or applicable to one particular geographical market why not nudge it along and use it as a test bed for new markets for your brand or service?

Another thing that this campaign highlights is the power of social media, and of digital channels in general, to transcend traditional boundaries like geography and time zones to reach a truly global audience… and all with the investment of nothing more than imagination and a little bit of time.

African children benefiting from the celebrity endorsed Twitter campaign to help eradicate malaria.

Links to campaign creative

External links:

- Video overview of the Twitter campaign: http://www.youtube.com/watch?v=ZADez_MIr5l;

- Malaria No More Website: http://www.malarianomore.org/news/features/world_malaria_day_world_malaria_day__april_25__2

- Malaria No More Buzzwords blog: http://malarianomore.org/blog/?tag=world-malaria-day

- Note from Ashton Kutcher on Facebook: http://www.facebook.com/note.php?note_id=68424669485

- Twitter: http://www.retweetradar.com/archived?id=20090425

Coverage:

- CNN: http://www.cnn.com/2009/TECH/04/17/ashton.cnn.twitter.battle/index.html

- Mashable: http://mashable.com/2009/04/25/world-malaria-day/

- Late Night with Jimmy Fallon: http://www.latenightwithjimmyfallon.com/blogs/2009/04/im-on-the-net-in-a-net/

- Oprah.com: http://www.oprah.com/article/oprahshow/20090417-tows-ashton-kutcher-twitter/5

- People.com: http://www.people.com/people/article/0,,20273244,00.html

- AdAge: http://adage.com/mediaworks/article?article_id=136532

Credits

Client	• Malaria No More
Geographical scope	• Global
Agencies	• Katalyst Media
Campaign contacts	• CEO/Vice Chairman: Timothy 'Scott' Case
Awards	• Think Social Awards: Nominee

Creative biography

Timothy 'Scott' Case

Scott Case with some of the Malaria No More campaign beneficiaries.

Timothy 'Scott' Case is a technologist, entrepreneur and inventor and was co-founder of priceline.com, the 'Name Your Own Price' internet service. As chief technology officer, he was responsible for building the technology that enabled priceline.com's hyper-growth. Moving beyond technology he successfully launched several priceline.com businesses. These included Priceline for Gasoline, by far the firm's fastest-growing business. At the Walker Digital Invention Laboratory, Scott helped build a portfolio of intellectual property, and is a named inventor on dozens of US patents including the underlying portfolio for priceline.com. Previously, Scott co-founded Precision Training Software, a software company that developed the world's first PC-based simulated flight instructor and photo-realistic flight simulator.

In 2006, Scott joined the Malaria No More team to inspire individuals and institutions in the private sector to end deaths cause by malaria. He also serves as the Chairman of Network for Good, a national non-profit organization that has distributed more than US $400 million to 50,000 causes around the world. Network for Good provides online fund-raising and communications services to over 5,000 non-profit organizations. Scott continues to build social enterprises that use technology, commercial processes and incentives to create sustainable, scalable solutions to improve people's lives.

CASE STUDY 24

BREAK THE CYCLE

The challenge

In a society where children are increasingly being demonized, the UK children's charity Barnardo's supports some of the UK's most troubled children. The charity wanted to raise awareness of how it works to help and support children by delivering cut-through and deepening engagement with its core target market. The charity wanted to create a campaign that would stand out and grab attention in an increasingly competitive sector, showing it in a contemporary light, while simultaneously bolstering 'deservedness'.

Target audience

ABC1 adults and the media.

Action

Barnardo's decided to launch the campaign in two separate phases. For the first phase they created a viral film called 'Hunting', a short piece that was seeded online. The film took real comments about children left by readers on newspaper websites and put them into the mouths of suburbanite adults with shotguns as they stalked their prey: the children. The idea behind the film was to attack the notion that discrimination against children is somehow acceptable. By targeting the key media and opinion leaders the team fostered a growing debate around the topics raised by the film.

The second phase of the campaign was designed to build on the discussion generated by the first phase, and to cast Barnardo's in the role of providing a solution to the problem of problematic children: that they could – and should – be helped rather than vilified. With this in mind, the team created a series of films (*Jail* / *Break the Cycle* / *What We Hear*) which start by confirming the stereotype of a troubled child, complete with aggressive and violent behaviour. As the films develop, viewers are slowly shown the other side to the same child: the side characterized by painful vulnerability. The intention was to expose the tension between these two different sides in order to force viewers to stop thinking in absolutes and start seeing troubled teens as children in dire need of support.

The interactive format of the films intensifies engagement: with a click of their mouse the online audience can switch between the two sides – listen to what an aggressive girl is really saying, lend their support to a troubled young-offender, step in and break a young girl's cycle of abuse. The interactive digital films ran as full-screen HD ads – a first for this medium, creating huge impact in the online environment.

The campaign aimed to raise a debate in wider society and show how, even after others have given up, Barnardo's still believes in the most troubled children.

Results

The online campaign had an interaction rate of 3.66 per cent across both the industry and charity sectors (well above industry average) with a very high replay rate. The engagement time was also higher than average across these two sectors.

Those who consumed the digital films had a stronger perception of the work Barnardo's does. Those who watched the digital films were significantly more likely to donate with an increase of 45 per cent. The 'Hunting' film helped to stimulate a debate around the demonization of children in the media, and resulted in several pieces of high-profile press coverage.

The campaign gave Barnardo's an opportunity to give the public true insight into our work. The creativity of the interactive ads, combined with the powerful images of the young people shown, enabled us to present the complex issues we face every day, in a compelling and engaging way.

Collette Collins, Assistant Director of Communications, Brand and New Media, Barnardo's.

Lessons

Video is a highly compelling and engaging medium that continues its explosive growth online. It's also a great way to provoke a response and encourage debate around a topic, which is how Barnardo's used it so effectively in this campaign. While the Barnardo's films were professionally produced, the barriers to entry for online video are incredibly low – and some of the most-viewed videos on video-sharing networks like YouTube and Vimeo are created with little more than a standard webcam or a relatively inexpensive digital video camera. It can be an incredibly effective, and cost-effective way to engage with a potentially massive audience, either as a stand-alone vehicle for your campaign, or more likely to augment an integrated campaign spanning multiple media channels.

Marketers, we all remember the days when the internet was criticized for being too unemotional and 'flat'. Creatives didn't like the restrictions and sometimes dismissed the medium on the basis that 'banner ads don't make you cry'. This campaign proves that digital has gone beyond other media – not only can it evoke emotion but its power to engage and stimulate more discussion and interaction is simply unmatched by any other medium we have ever encountered.

Also note the increased level of contributions – up by 45 per cent. When it comes to 'giving' it is useful to know that internet users are usually a more affluent audience with access to credit cards thereby reducing the barriers to return on investment (ROI).

One of the Barnardo's ads running on the *Guardian* website – clicking on the ad switched to the full-screen HD experience.

Links to campaign creative

- http://creativity-online.com/work/barnardos-hunted/1
- http://www.grazeourfield.com/barnardos/troubledyouth/

Credits

Client	● Barnardo's
Geographical scope	● UK
Agencies	● N/A
Campaign contacts	● Assistant Director of Communications (Brand and New Media): Collette Collins
Awards	● Creative Circle: Gold
	● Andy Awards: Gold
	● British Television Awards: Silver
	● D&AD: Digital
	● Cannes Lion: Gold (Digital)

Creative biography

Collette Collins

As the Assistant Director of Communications Collette is responsible for coordinating Barnardo's brand and new media campaigns. Before joining Barnardo's she worked in advertising, developing brand communication on several major UK and international brands.

CASE STUDY 25

BARACK OBAMA 2008 PRESIDENTIAL CAMPAIGN – THE 15 SWING STATES

The challenge

Two months before the presidential election of 2008, Barack Obama's campaign needed to reach out to voters in 15 critical swing states. They looked to Pontiflex for a cost-effective way to collect the contact information of interested voters and potential campaign donors.

Campaign budget

US $137,000 on interactive CPL (cost per lead) display ads with Pontiflex over a six-week period.

Target audience

Crucial voters in 15 swing states that would determine the outcome of the presidential election.

Action

This crucial portion of the presidential election campaign ran various interactive sign-up ads across prominent online destinations as part of a three-step performance branding programme. Here's how they did it.

Acquired contact information through high ROI display banners

The Obama campaign deployed a range of CPL ad units, including Pontiflex AdUnit X interactive banners: high-ROI (return on investment) display ads that allowed them to collect contact information from within the ads themselves. That meant there was no need for users to click through to a landing page to submit their information, resulting in vastly improved conversion rates and increased returns on ad spend. The campaign paid only for actual leads generated, not for clicks or impressions.

Engaged through e-mail

Sending timely e-mails to potential voters and donors was a key component of Obama's marketing strategy. By communicating regularly through a newsletter programme, the campaign was able to maintain a steady stream of messages to an audience base that (because they opted in through the CPL sign-up ads) was predisposed to pay attention.

Branded in relevant ways

In addition to using it as a tool for information sharing, the Obama campaign also used e-mail to direct voters and donors to multiple engagement vehicles:

Facebook pages, social communities, donation pages, Twitter forums, YouTube videos and mobile apps.

Results

The campaign achieved high open and click-through rates for its automated follow-up e-mails. Driven by sustained and timely e-mails and word of mouth, the campaign received extremely high levels of engagement through social networks and online communities.

The Obama iTunes app had more than 30,000 messages. The campaign's Facebook page had more than 3 million supporters; and the Twitter account garnered more than 100,000 followers.

The ultimate result, of course, was a historical presidential victory for Barack Obama.

Lessons

The Obama campaign has been widely lauded as a masterclass in online political marketing and engagement, and will, no doubt, form a blueprint for future campaigns both in the US and around the world. One of the key lessons from this particular portion of the campaign, which focused on the critical 'swing states', is one that resonates across all disciplines of online marketing and indeed any kind of online business you're engaged in. It's simply this: keeping things simple will improve conversion. Remove obstacles and reduce the number of steps a user has to take to do what you want them to do, and more of them are likely do it.

Increasing conversion is the most effective way of boosting return on your online investment. Keep things as simple as they can possibly be for the user – to check out of your online shopping cart, to sign up for your newsletter, to subscribe to your RSS feed – and you'll improve your results.

Getting the performance of your landing pages right can be a major hurdle when you're looking to optimize online conversion. But by integrating the sign-up process into interactive display ad units for this portion of the campaign, the Obama team cleverly sidestepped that pitfall. Because users weren't forced to leave the page they were interested in to sign up, they were much more inclined to submit their information and then simply pick up where they left off with the content of the page. Simple, efficient and devastatingly effective!

Marketers, although it is some time since this campaign took place and Obama was sworn in, there is a lasting message from this work and it is this: start with digital in mind – break the traditional way of thinking first. Do not listen to agencies who tramp in with the usual 'reach and frequency' models and standard media schedules on which many are dependent for their financial livelihood. Get your team around the table and forbid anyone from discussing any other channel other than digital. Once that is achieved then address the rest of it.

For too many years digital has been a virtual 'afterthought' of the typical agency solution to a client's problem. The great change brought about by the Obama campaign represented a paradigm shift that was long overdue. By placing digital first and allowing the competition to resort to the usual, conventional and tired methods of distribution… yes you can!

Links to campaign creative

- http://www.pontiflex.com/landing/obamacampaign.jsf
- http://www.clickz.com/3632263

Credits

Client	● Barack Obama
Geographical scope	● United States
Agencies	● Pontiflex
Campaign contacts	● Chief Revenue Officer: Jon Beardsley
Awards	● The overall Obama 2008 digital campaign, of which this CPL element was a key part, has won numerous industry awards, including the coveted 'Titanium Grand Prix' and 'Integrated Grand Prix' at the esteemed Cannes Lions advertising awards.

Creative biography

Jon Beardsley

Jon Beardsley, Chief Revenue Officer, Pontiflex.

Simply put, Jon makes Pontiflex grow. He's a master of all verticals, with major sales successes in travel, retail, technology, education, non-profit and market research. His greatest triumph was securing the Barack Obama presidential campaign as a client after almost two years of perseverance.

Before Pontiflex Jon held a series of leadership roles at Innovation Ads, a premier interactive agency. He helped his department grow 20-fold and was instrumental in the company being named the 29th-fastest-growing small business in America, as named by *Entrepreneur Magazine* and PricewaterhouseCoopers. Back in the day: Jon worked for Britain's new local government network and taught kids how to unleash vicious forehands at tennis camps at Harvard.

When not thinking about CPL Jon is dedicated to charitable causes in Africa, with a specific focus on Liberia. He has been involved in The Grassroots Movement of Liberia and the rebuilding of the war-torn city of Monrovia.

LOOKING FORWARD TO A CREATIVE DIGITAL FUTURE

'Genesis and Revelations, the next generation will be... hear me.'

Police and Thieves (originally Junior Murvin, mastered by The Clash)

Creativity dictates our future. The power to imagine through storytelling can unlock global change as well as filling the coffers of brave digital marketers everywhere by pushing the boundaries of what we understand to be the norm. If this book has taught us anything it is this: that nobody knows the boundaries, nobody knows just how far we can go in the future with digital marketing. All we now know is that the rules change on a continual basis, standards of excellence are breached daily and the future looks bright.

One of the many problems we now have of course is defining 'what is digital?' In fact we would suggest we are now beyond the point of 'reasonable distinction'. Instead perhaps we can just move up a gear, and assume all marketing is digital, as it's hard to think of a single reason why an advertiser wouldn't deploy at least one digital aspect within a campaign. That's simply because we can all safely accept today that at least some of our audience is going to want to engage with us online.

This chapter is going to summarize the book. We are trying to knit some themes together, analyse what is actually going on and present it to you in a reasonably intelligent manner. We are also going to make some predictions about the future for creativity in digital and advertising as a whole. After all that, we are going to offer some recommendations for advertisers.

But first a quick recap of from whence we came.

In the beginning there were banners, and they probably didn't please many, but like our ancient friends from the traditional press who spent several hundred years lumping ink and trees around the place to form similarly offensive advertisements, it just took some time to get it right.

Banners have fought hard to remain on the schedule. They flashed, buzzed, expanded, contracted, floated, popped up and under, in and out, and generally sought to intrude while howling 'CLICK ME' at the growing billions online.

On the second day the internet had a God and Google was its name. Although 'search' had been around for some time and indeed keywords were nothing new, it was Google who got it right through advanced algorithms and its saintly, 'do no evil' image. Now advertisers didn't have to rely on banners for response and traffic, they could simply de-risk the process by acquiring disciples who were already looking for answers.

Improvements in broadband brought us video – now we could choose between being passive or interactive. We could also wrap around, pre-roll, post-roll, take over and do lots of other neat stuff as we marched happily towards the dawn of convergence. However, we were still caught inside the boundaries of a site or destination and our clicks and strokes were somewhat victims of circumstance and distraction. Then two key trends emerged and we found ourselves on the brink of a new horizon; the beginning of the user-generated content era or Web 2.0 or let's just call it 'social'; and the other major trend was, of course, 'mobile'.

Mobile has been quite a drawn-out and at times hilarious journey. I remember the times when I was commuting in the UK (circa 1989) and someone would be on their giant phone: 'Hi, yeah, I'm on a train, yeah, I might lose you as a tunnel is coming up', and all the other passengers would 'tut tut' and shuffle their morning papers around. Now the 'tutting' has become 'tapping' and some of the morning papers are handed out free of charge. There is no doubt we are getting closer to the device of choice for the Web 3.0 or Web 4.0 generation; iPhone and iPad have gone some way towards this but the best is surely yet to come.

So back to our gospel. Then the conversation opened up for all, advertisers included. No more would we be servants of the net, we would be authors, film directors, political leaders, visionaries, champions, fashionistas, rock stars clicking in a levelled world earning our 15 gigabytes of fame. For those more ordinary folk, we too would be empowered in the most extraordinary ways – here we are reminded of the great legend and media prophet of the 20th century, Marshall McLuhan. For those of you who haven't heard of the man, he is well worth a 'search'. In fact, McLuhan was the under-riding inspiration for our first book *Understanding Digital Marketing*. If you have ever come across a really witty or insightful quote from the world of media and advertising, chances are it was McLuhan who quipped it. Our favourites include:

- Good taste is the first refuge of the non-creative. It is the last ditch stand of the artist.
- The modern little red riding hood, reared on singing commercials has no objection to being eaten by the wolf!
- Today it's not the classroom nor the classics which are the repositories of models of eloquence , but the ad agencies.
- Diaper backward spells repaid.

McLuhan observed that the successful adoption of new media by societies followed four basic principles or qualifiers – called a 'tetrad'. It is a very useful qualifier for new stuff like 'social media'.

Ad, fad, mad or tetrad?

What is enhanced?

McLuhan argues a new media must have global impact and enhance what was there before. Social clearly provides power to the collective in a whole new way. The contents of this book make that obvious.

What is obsolesced?

Postcards? Letter writing? Perhaps these two types of messaging are actually going to be more valued in the future as a result, but one clear question from this book is whether or not individuals require power to achieve authority. Is it, in fact, the getting of power that is being obsolesced by social media?

What has this new medium borrowed from media already made obsolete?

The days of having a pen pal seem long gone – is that what has happened here? Pen-pal protocol has been dusted off and relaunched as social media? Or do we go further back to the fireside and the born-again art of storytelling?

What will this new medium reverse into?

In our last book we predicted the rise of the personal search engine. We also predicted the creation of celebrity search engines. Perhaps we have yet to see the medium that will encompass all of the above or maybe it is already chiming in our pocket bursting to be reversed into – consequently we don't see any point in testing whether or not mobile is going to be a commercial success, do you?

So here we are, busy dispensing with old media stuff like telephones and cables, and unshackling ourselves to explore this new world. Mobiles are now our constant sidekicks, helping us stay connected and engaged with the world, and as we already heard at the start of this book, access to the internet via a PC will be superseded by mobiles by 2013.

For advertisers and their creative advisors quite a bit has happened in the space of about 10 years. But back to our case studies...

Summarizing the case studies

In no particular order, we have read how mobile applications are helping Dockers to sell clobber and Pizza Hut to involve their eaters in the creation of their chosen feasts. We saw how Mercedes used digital to promote its Smart car, although I am not sure why anyone would challenge the notion that the car is small, but strong enough to withstand the force of 400 elephants – I would have enjoyed watching that test!

We checked out Doritos scaring the life out of young munchers by integrating them into their personal horror films and mused on Lynx's assault on the senses (scents?) of Australians – incidentally check out the media schedule for this case study; times have changed.

We had Simon Cowell and his Christmas number one ambition thwarted by digital as the nation rallied behind Rage Against the Machine and a song so full of expletives that I'm fu**ed if I can remember the title. Those intrepid lads in Lean Mean Fighting Machine then showed us how to bring some real meaning to Samsung via Nick Turpin's photo diaries.

It might seem obvious to use social media to get Obama into power, but promoting online tax returns was a pretty smart move, congrats to TurboTax.

E-mail made an appearance courtesy of Rice Krispies as Kellogg's targeted US mums with some rather nifty creative. We then saw an increased use of celebrityism with Kanye West engaging with Absolut Vodka (I know the feeling) and Ashton Kutcher leading Ophrah Winfrey and others to support World Malaria Day. This was truly one of the more heart-warming stories in the book – more than US $500,000 raised via Twitter alone and almost 90,000 mosquito nets sent to help those less fortunate.

Digital media continues to show its mettle in this area – check out SMS For Life campaign and see how mobile technology is saving lives in Tanzania and other parts of the world. Another campaign showing how digital can help others is Barnado's, a truly brilliant example of how interactive video can engage an audience.

We loved Wario Land's campaign for its new Wii game. Instead of using a page takeover they went for a page destroyer and let the games' characters decimate the screen for those inclined. That brings us swiftly on to 'rich media'... how rich exactly? Stinking! Take a look at what AvatarLabs produced for movies *Star Trek* and *WALL-E*.

The Australian theme continued to feature prominently throughout the research – Foster's and its concept of 'shadow napping' became practically a social phenomenon while, from the same amber nectar, we encountered 'The Ozometer', a cool online application designed to measure your level of 'no worries'. Perhaps we should test that on our publisher!

We didn't expect to see IBM play a role, but its campaign to keep software projects on track certainly made the cut, as did fellow techies Nokia, who showed how to cultivate and engage with an audience resulting in the creation of more than 30,000 widgets for its N97 phone.

Art played a role, however subjective you may feel that is, or isn't, or is! See the case studies from Frankfurt as the city was engaged in a digital art project and read of our Portuguese cousins who convinced Pampero Rum to get behind another alternative art project.

Of course no book on digital marketing success would be complete without some reference to the ground-breaking Obama election (recommended read for the full story, *Yes We Did* by Rahaf Harfoush).

Finally we had campaigns as diverse as Pepsi enticing Turkish women to text and win, and Radiohead using digital in an amazing way to promote their Japanese music tour.

In summary, digital applies to all brands, all markets, all target audiences and there is really no excuse not to be on board. Social media and mobile are clearly the two rising stars joining the mighty 'search' and other media, but the really exciting difference now is the attention and emphasis advertisers place on investment in creative. The results are clear and plain to see. The other exciting trend to watch in the next few years is the 'return of display'. Recent technical innovations by companies such as www.struq.com mean advertisers are seeing better performances from display than search! Watch that space… display is now growing faster than search for the first time.

Whereas digital got out of the starting blocks by being accountable, cheap to produce and cheap to distribute, we are now in the middle of a creative burst of energy as the world's brands and agencies seek to push deeper and wider to evoke change.

That for us was the key theme emanating from this work – digital creates real *change*. In behaviour, in consciousness, in depth of engagement, in awareness and in buy-in. Whether that 'buy-in' takes the form of sales, votes, samples, downloads, enquiries, prospects or just the commitment of time to engage with a brand – this stuff works.

Just ask Ben Southall, winner of the 'Best Job in the World' campaign whereby Queensland Tourism achieved awareness among three billion people of an opportunity for one person to become a paid caretaker on an island in the Great Barrier Reef for a year – what a change that was.

So what about the future of advertising and the future of creativity?

If there is one reason to invest in creative it is this. Clutter. Like the billions of stars in the sky, if your message is to shine brightest among the billions of messages it needs careful and appropriate investment. This shouldn't dissuade smaller advertisers from taking part in this firmament, we have already seen in this book how some campaigns have achieved digital marketing success for a relatively small budget.

Years ago it may have been OK to drop a few dollars on some flashy banners, but in this increasingly competitive environment we believe advertisers need to go the extra mile. Moreover, advertisers should be ensuring their media advisers are completely up to speed with the massively shifting audiences online and what is generating buzz and social adoption.

Why? Because like the speed of the expanding universe, the places in which we advertise are accelerating too. The media department of the future will be completely foreign to anything we know today. The emphasis will be on analysis, clients will access real-time reports on where their target audience is located and we don't mean just geographical location.

Advertisers will choose to follow their audience as they move from place to place – the shower radio in the morning, the drive to work, the download of apps, playing of games, shopping in the high street, landing at Heathrow – ubiquitous, intelligent and controllable messaging. Advertisers will understand the shift in behaviour, the increasing sense of fickleness between media – old social media sites being cast aside in favour of the latest new thing. Media brands that come and go, that can reinvent themselves on an ongoing basis; imagine media with no name – that is our destination, that is our future.

The level of control the consumer will display in the future makes today's challenges look easy. However, several ingredients and investment therein will ensure advertisers are in a stronger position to cope and compete.

Data

Advertisers and media need to understand the power of data. If 'creative' is the glue that binds everything together, data is the justification. It's the stuff that gets your chief financial officer to sign off a bigger budget than they are comfortable with because you have the data and therefore the power to back it up. Understand your audience, but being able to measure this with reliable, meaningful and accurate data – that will be an investment worth your while.

We have been gathering data for years and have recently become quite adept with its power and management (ask Google). What we have yet to understand is the manipulation of the 'other data' – the things we think about and on which we do not act. Twitter has gone some way to release the randomness of thought. The great challenge surely has to be how to harvest and utilize this human data without crashing into the rock of privacy. Or is it our understanding of privacy that has to change or is already changing?

One thing I have noticed recently and have started to discuss with people is the everyday self-management of several online personalities: LinkedIn, Facebook and so on. Maybe we feel we need to be different people in different online environments, but doesn't that question one's credibility in some way? Anyway, as McLuhan said: 'I am here to explore not to explain'.

Our bet is those advertisers who understand as much data as can humanely and legally be obtained about their customers will be unassailable.

Agencies

Some may decide to do it themselves, and good luck to them. Others, including the vast majority of big brands, will usually select an agency. Picking the right agency, however, is becoming a far more complex and strategically important task. Why? Because successful agencies have evolved like the media they rely on and are increasingly becoming 'guardians of our customer engagement channel' rather than the guys who make our ads. I see successful agencies in the future being characterized by their level of investment in their clients rather than the other way around.

Put it another way; rather than pitching for the new US $1 million Acme Anoraks account, a future agency might decide to purchase 50,000 anoraks from Acme and seek exclusivity on media activity for a period of time, allowing it to cultivate its data, ignite its social media, mobile and search strategies and make a far superior margin by doing so. And lest we forget, agencies came into this world as sales representatives of space on behalf of newspapers – perhaps McLuhan's tetrad extends to agencies as well as media.

Forrester Research in its report on the future of agencies says:

Agencies continually reinvent themselves to serve their clients – they have to quickly adapt to changes in marketing strategy, media, technology, and society. And with the rise of social media and digital proliferation, we are entering an Adaptive Marketing era. In this era, mass media is no longer the foundation of marketing communication, forcing yet another change in the expectations of what marketing agencies can and should deliver. Marketers should assess their partners using the three Is – ideas, interaction, and intelligence – to select the right partners. Marketers who change their thinking will lay the groundwork for partners that are more agile, can build long-term relationships with active customers and communities, and can use data to drive real-time decisions.

Also worthy of a mention here is a piece of forthcoming research we are conducting with the UK's CAM Foundation. We are trying to measure how advertisers and agencies feel about the impact of technology and digital marketing, and what the world will look like in the year 2020. The research will be published in October 2010 and presented at the World Association of Marketing Agencies conference in Washington DC. Our thanks to Marialena Zinopoulou and her team at the CAM Foundation and Deb Geiger, Keith McCracken and Kieran Killeen of www.maaw.org.

Speed

Whether an advertiser uses an agency or not, speed to market and speed to respond will become instantaneous. In fact, we believe the minimum speed to react in the future has to be very very fast indeed. Perhaps using data to drive marketing, advertisers should be able to respond to world events and changing media habits in the blink of an eye. Think about the Tom Cruise movie *Minority Report* and remember how the outdoor ads changed depending on who was walking past. That's the sort of speed we need to achieve.

Some time ago we included an article on our website (www.understandingdigital.com) about how the adoption and abandonment of new media and new media brands are on an accelerated path. This means that popular digital destinations today can be disregarded in a flash tomorrow. Just think that Google, the biggest media company in the world (by market cap), is only 11 years old. Facebook is just six and as for Twitter… well the word 'meteoric' springs to mind. Now think that in several years' time we may rely on real-time reports that score the most logical places to engage customers based on data, some of which hasn't been created yet but presupposed on what the individual or the brand does to stimulate *thought*. This sounds like creative to me.

Creative

And I guess that is what this book was all about in the first place. We now know advertisers invest more in online creative than they used to – we can also see evidence that they (advertisers) are allowing more control into the hands of their target audiences than ever before. Our recommendation to advertisers is to *try everything*. Look beyond the market research, get over ancient obsessions with 'reach and frequency' models. Invest in respectful marketing that doesn't treat your audience like lemons – get them involved too.

Be wary of agencies that sell to you based on their ability to buy media cheaper than their foes. In fact, do your own 'digital audit' of an agency based on its social media footprint and its ranking in search engines too – if they genuinely 'get' digital, it will be all over it. Take part in the online discussion about you and find ways to play around with mobile. Playing is a great way to learn. I am told that most advertisers now want apps but don't know why – this is encouraging to hear.

Thanks for reading our book and thanks again to all those who took part in the discussion.

INDEX

NB: page numbers in *italic* indicate figures or illustrations/photographs

Also available from **Kogan Page**

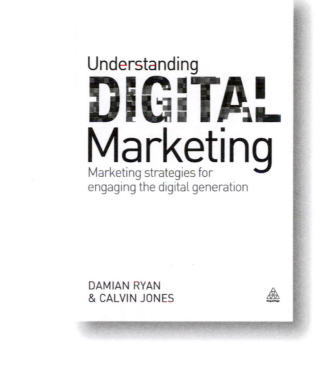

Understanding
DIGITAL
Marketing
Marketing strategies for
engaging the digital generation

**DAMIAN RYAN
& CALVIN JONES**

Find out more; visit **www.koganpage.com** and
sign up for offers and regular e-newsletters.

With over 42 years of publishing, more than 80 million people have succeeded in business with thanks to **Kogan Page**

www.koganpage.com

KoganPage